NUBA & LATUKA

George Rodger

NUBA & LATUKA

The Colour Photographs

Essays by Aaron Schuman and
Chris Steele-Perkins

PRESTEL
MUNICH · LONDON · NEW YORK

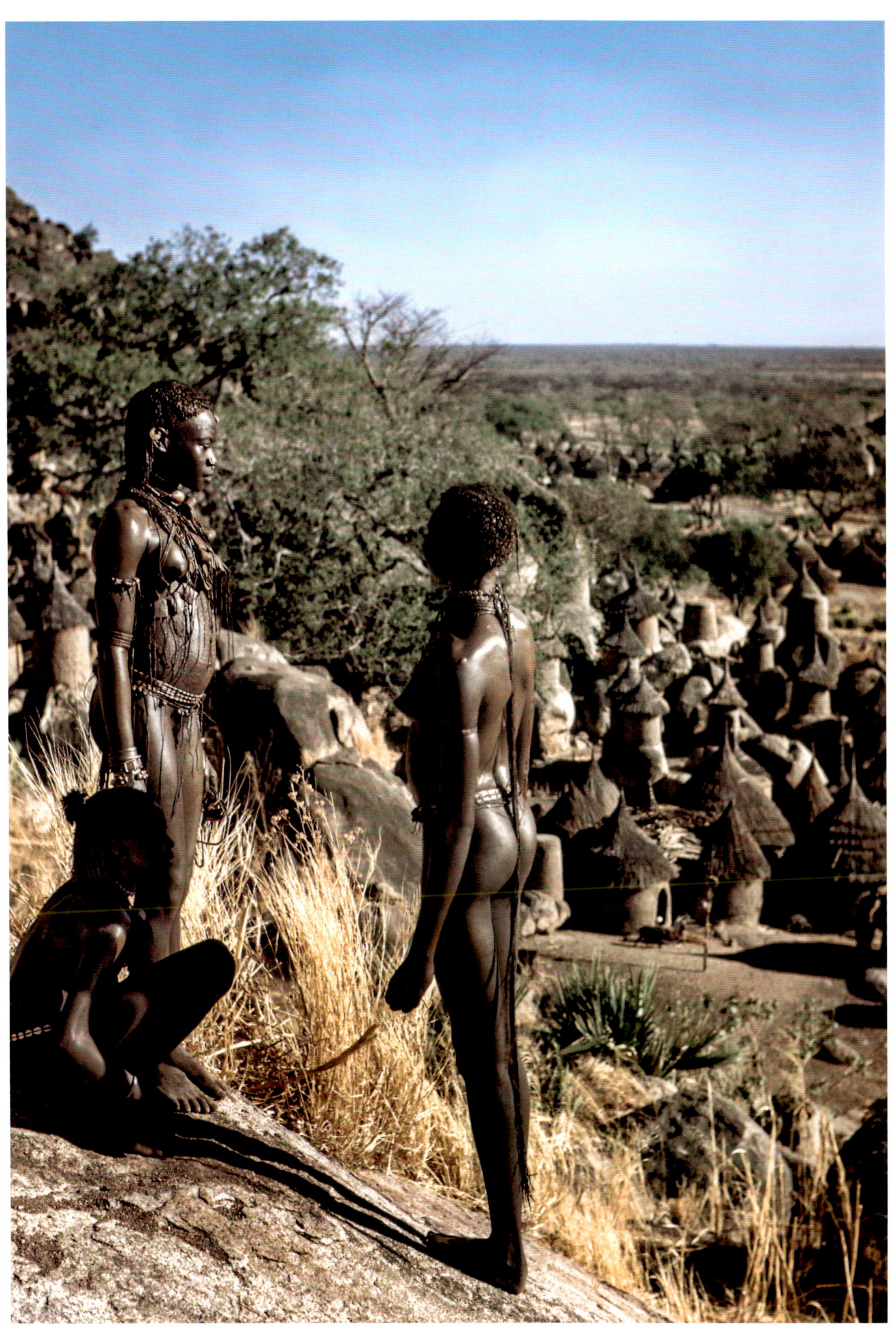

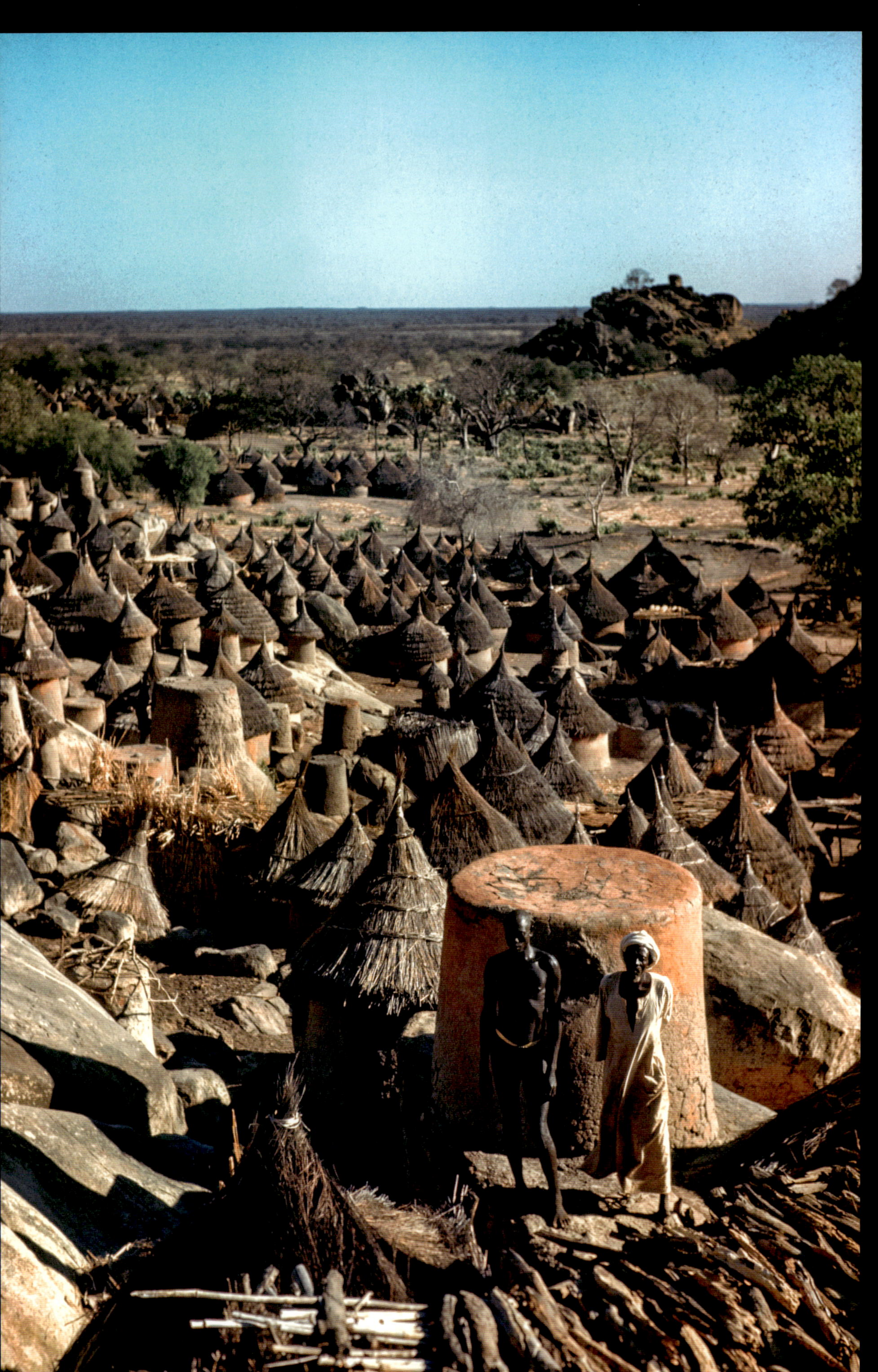

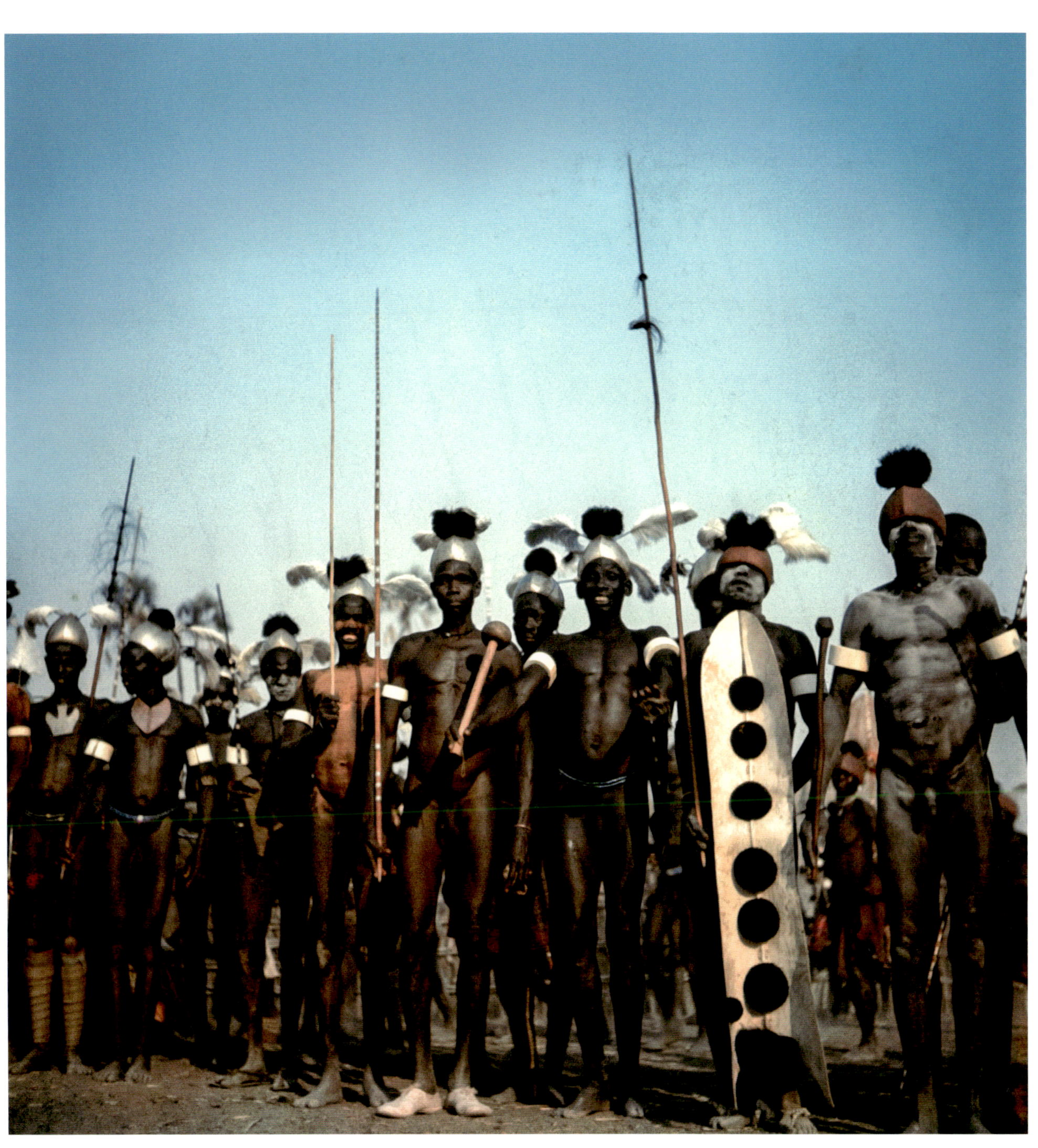

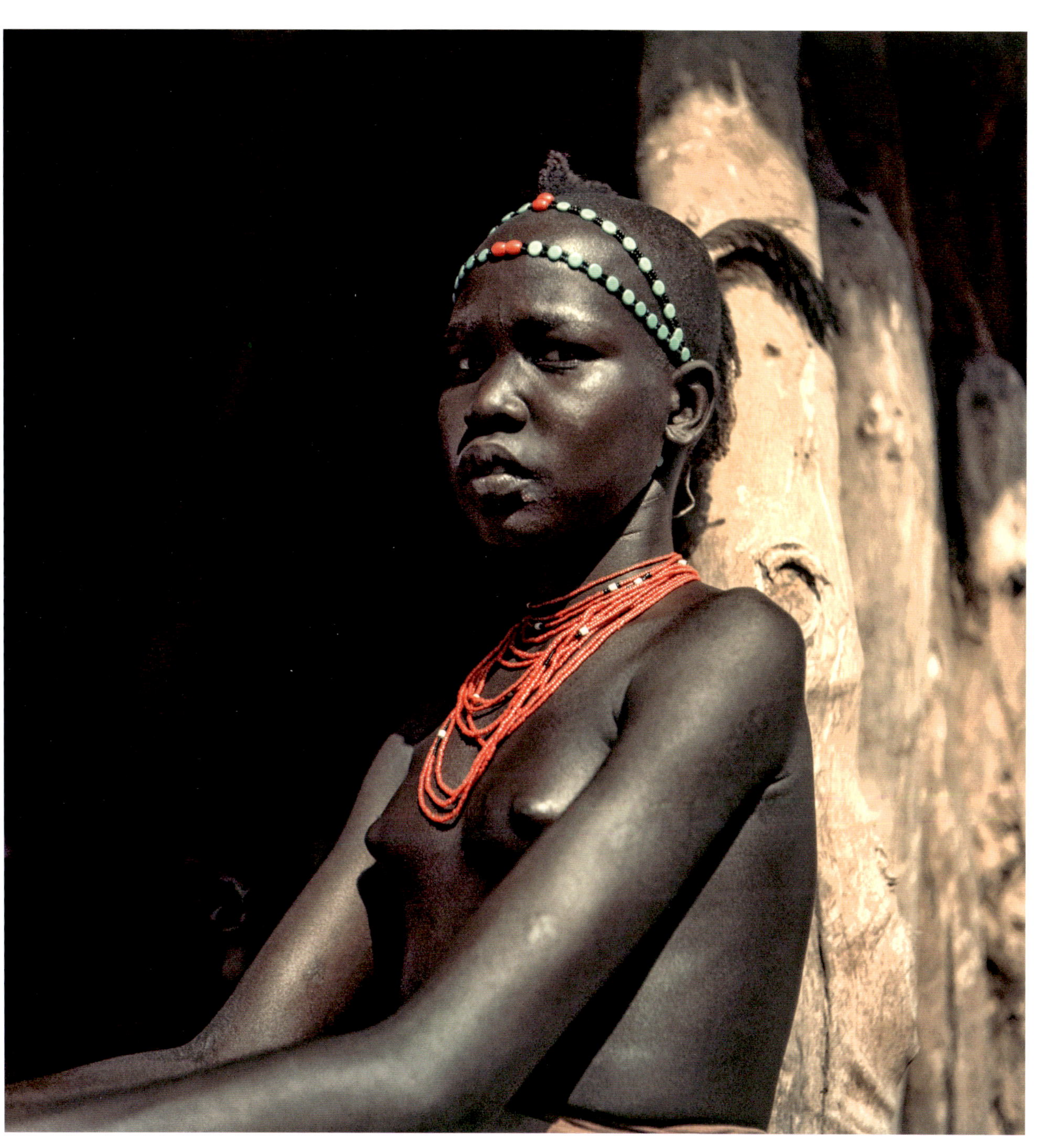

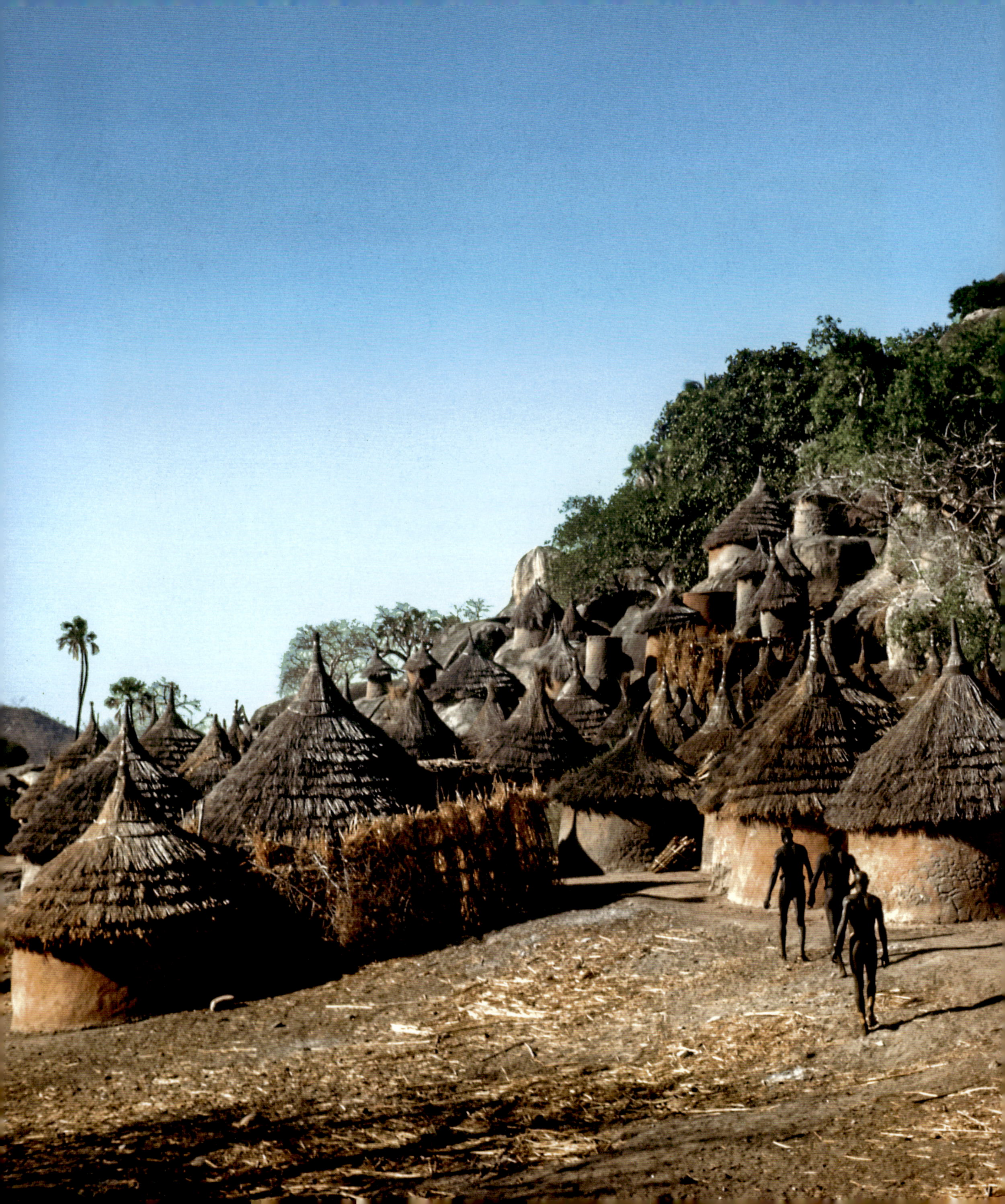

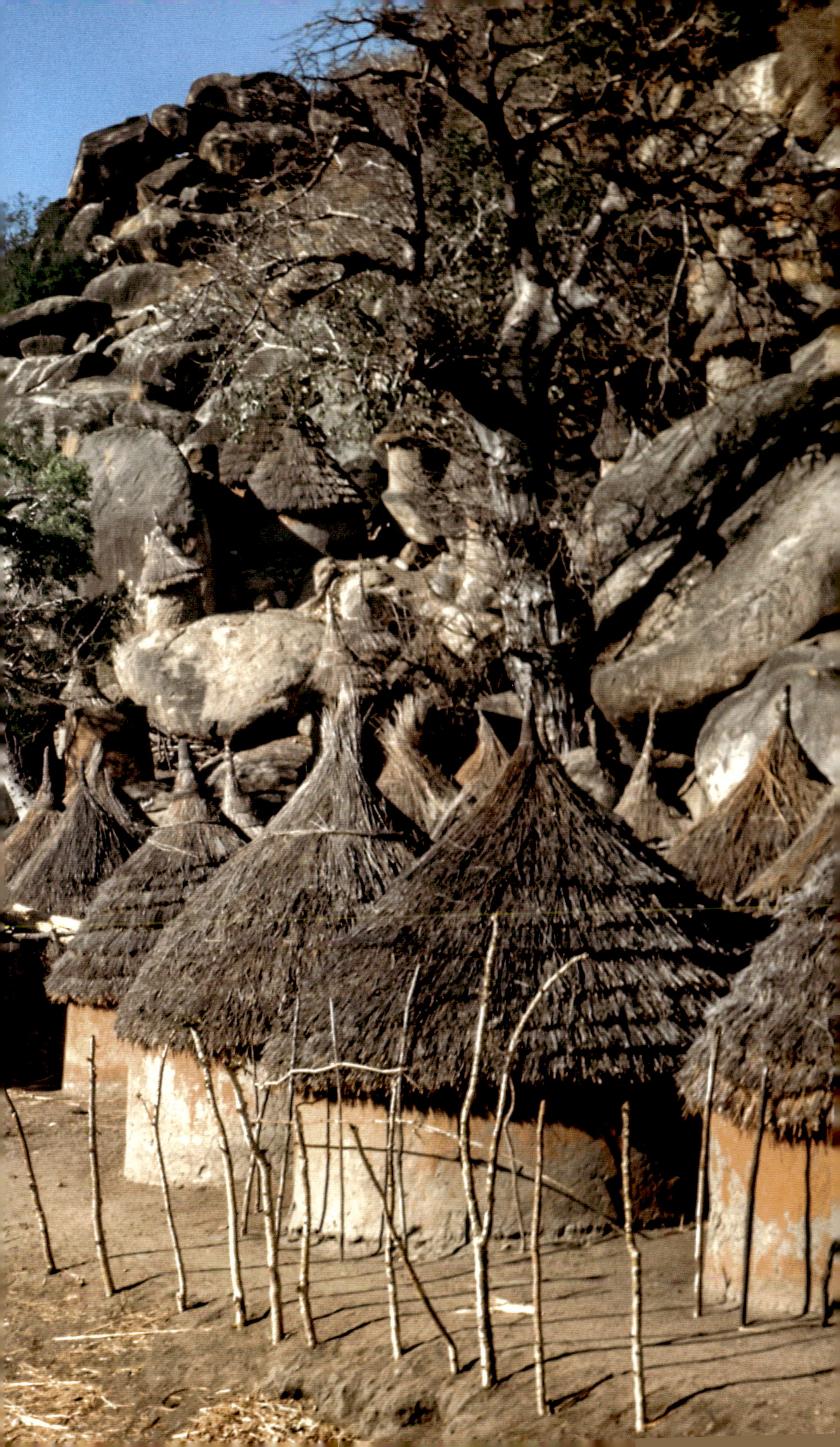

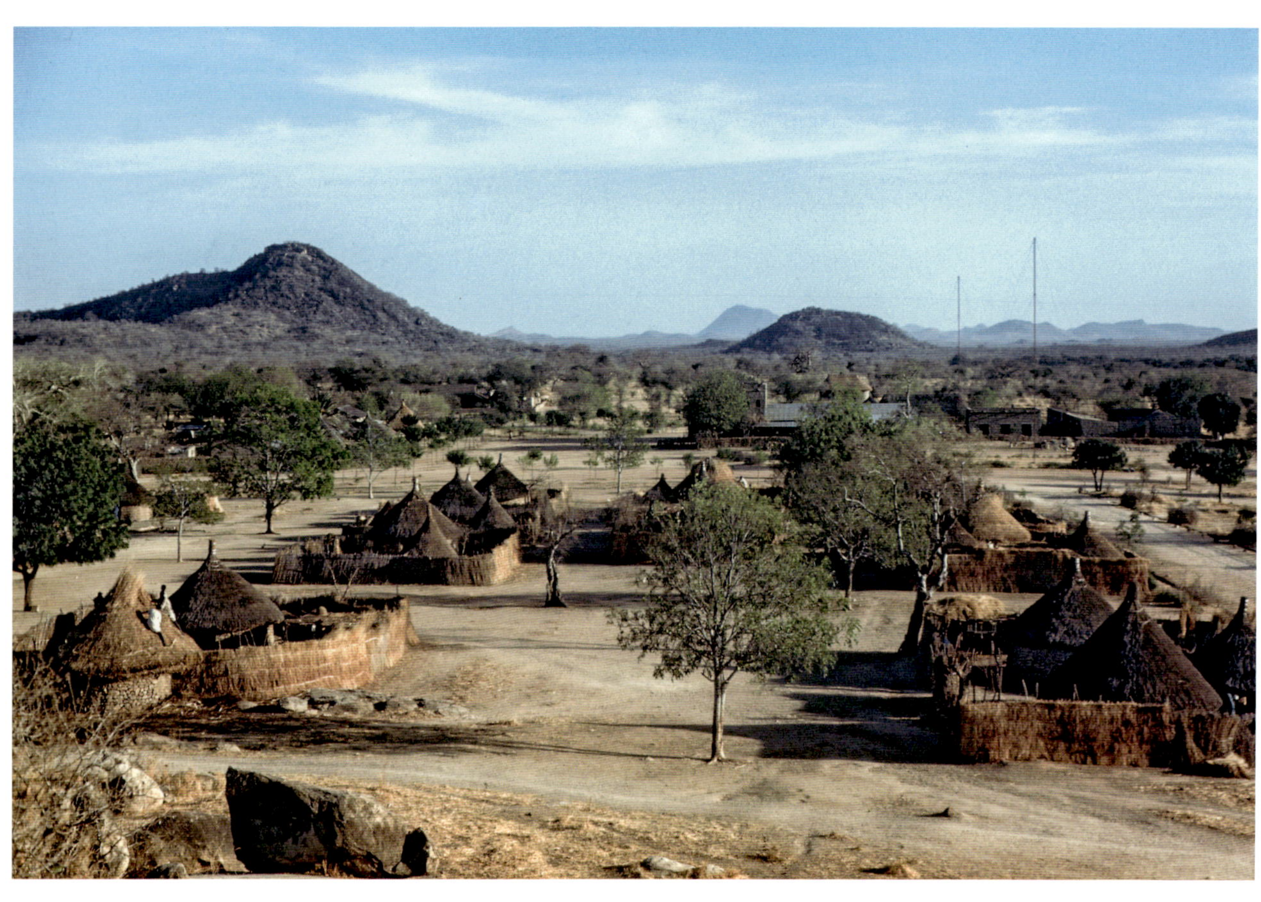

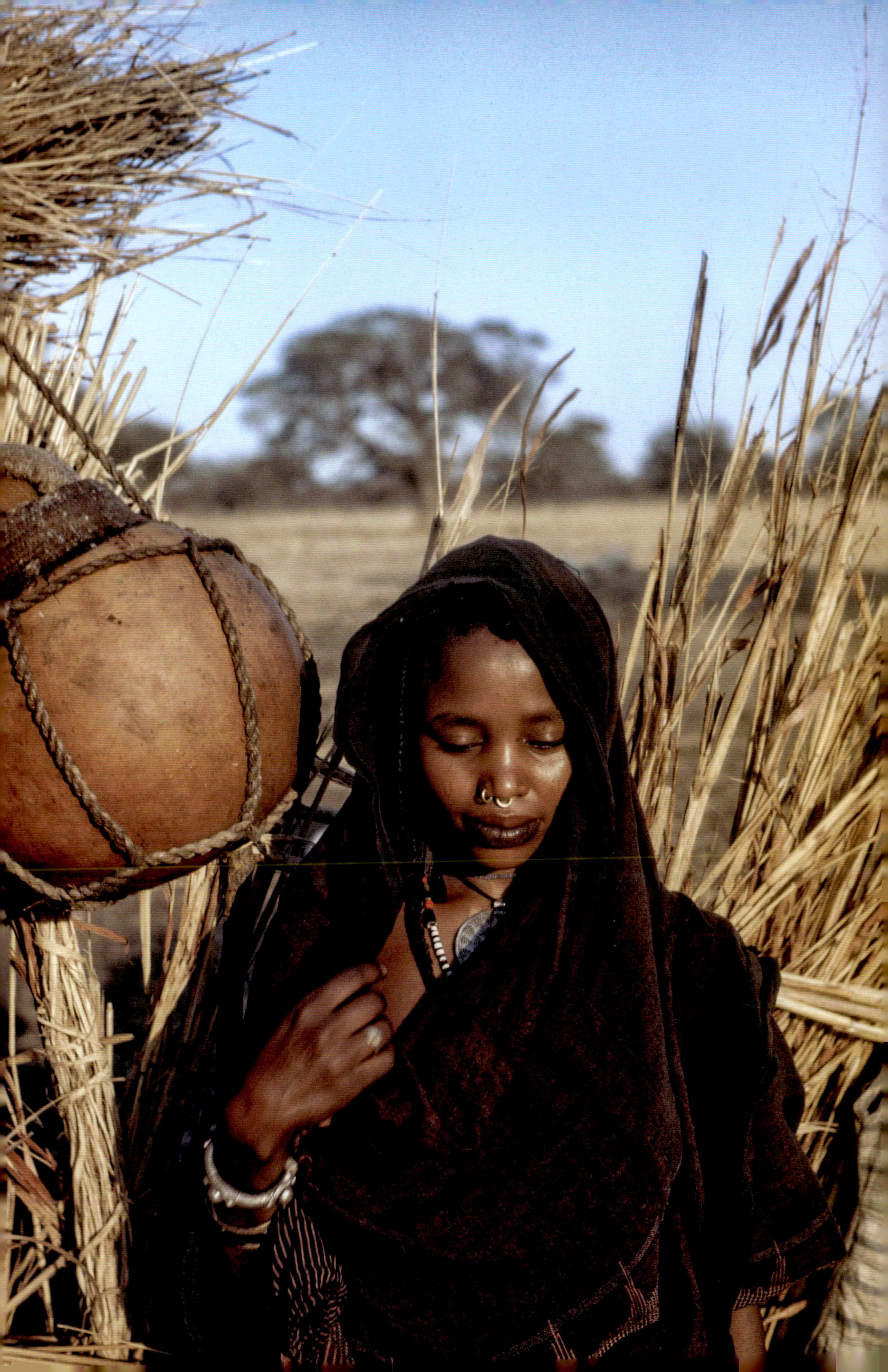

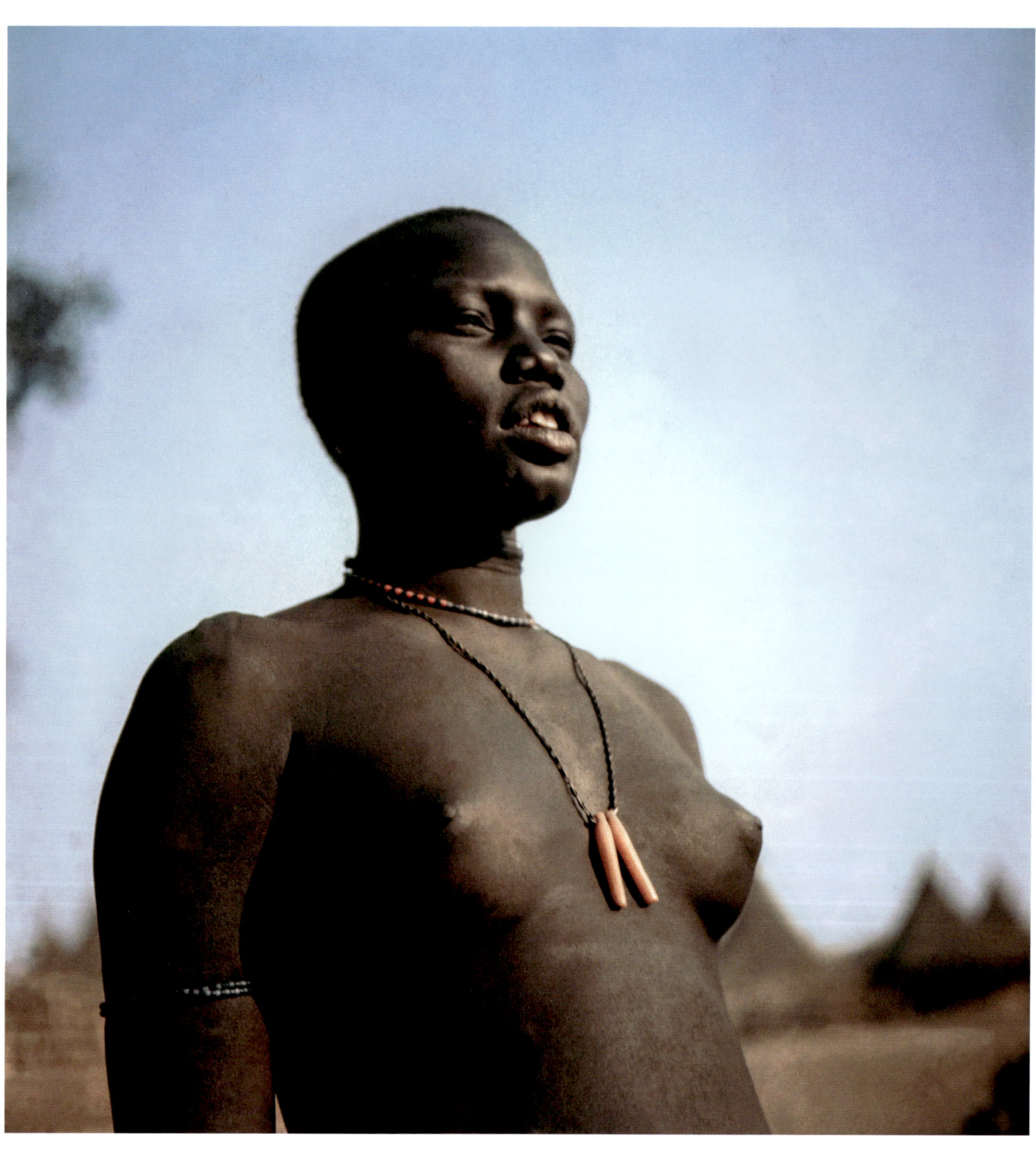

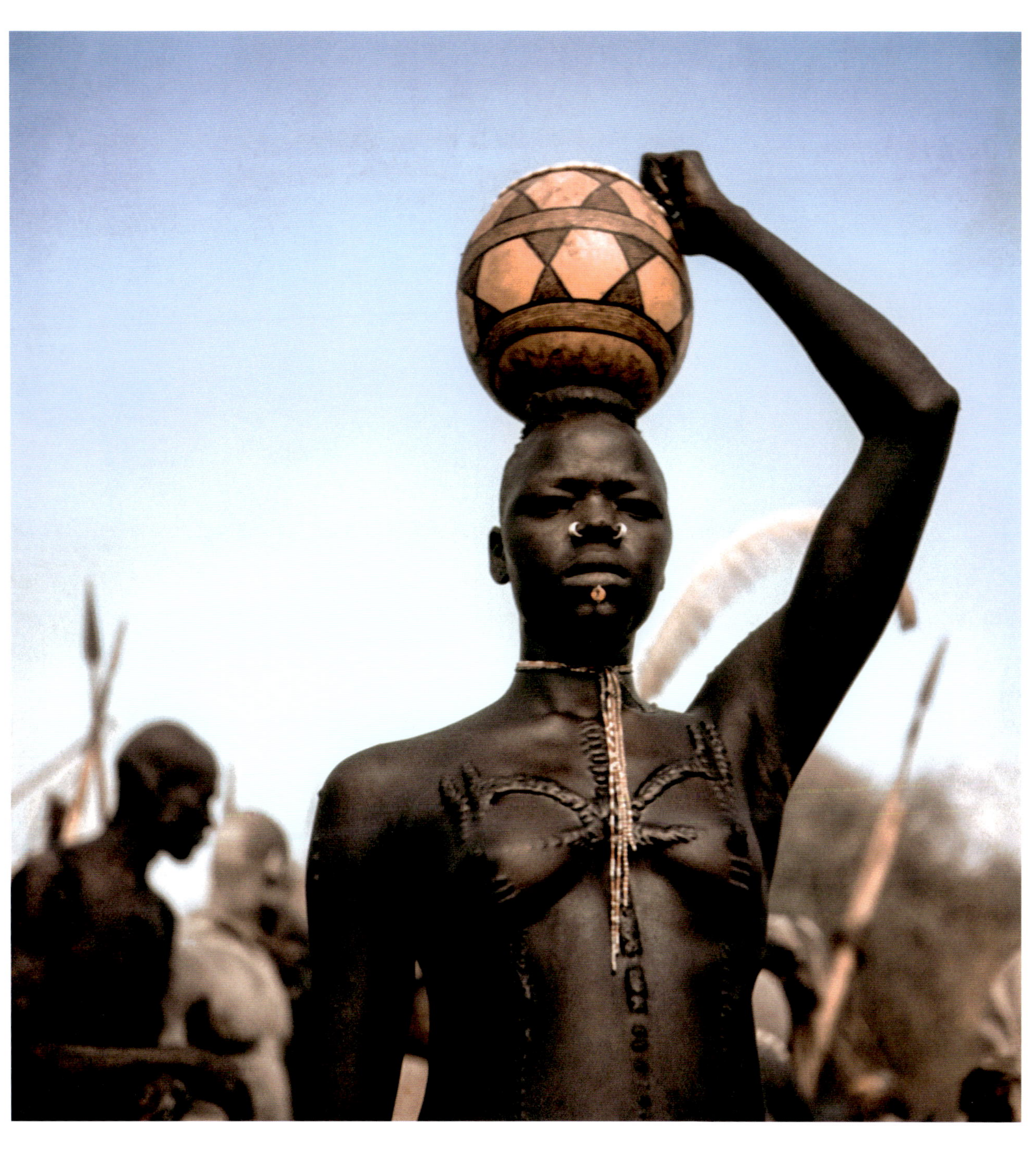

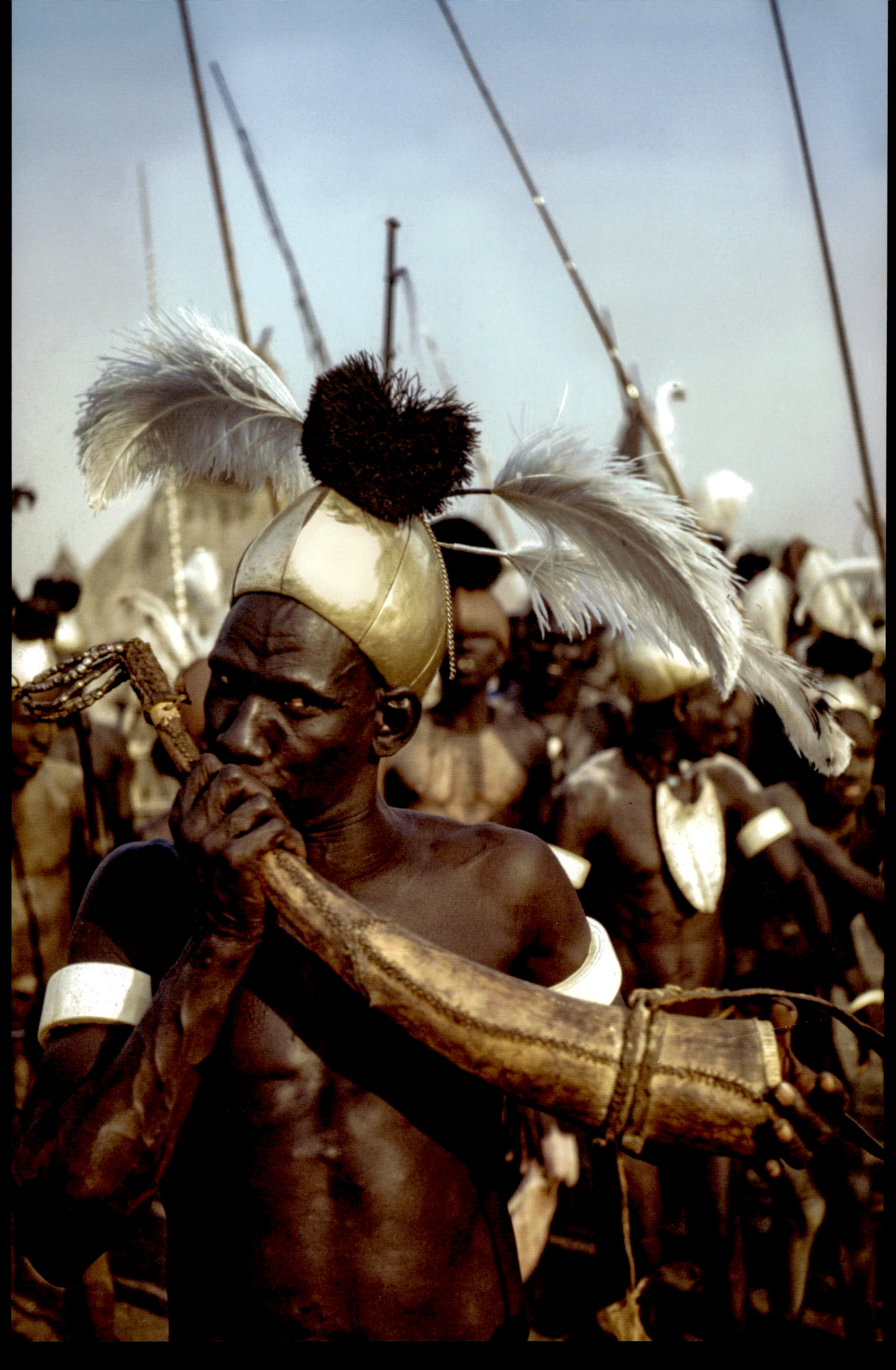

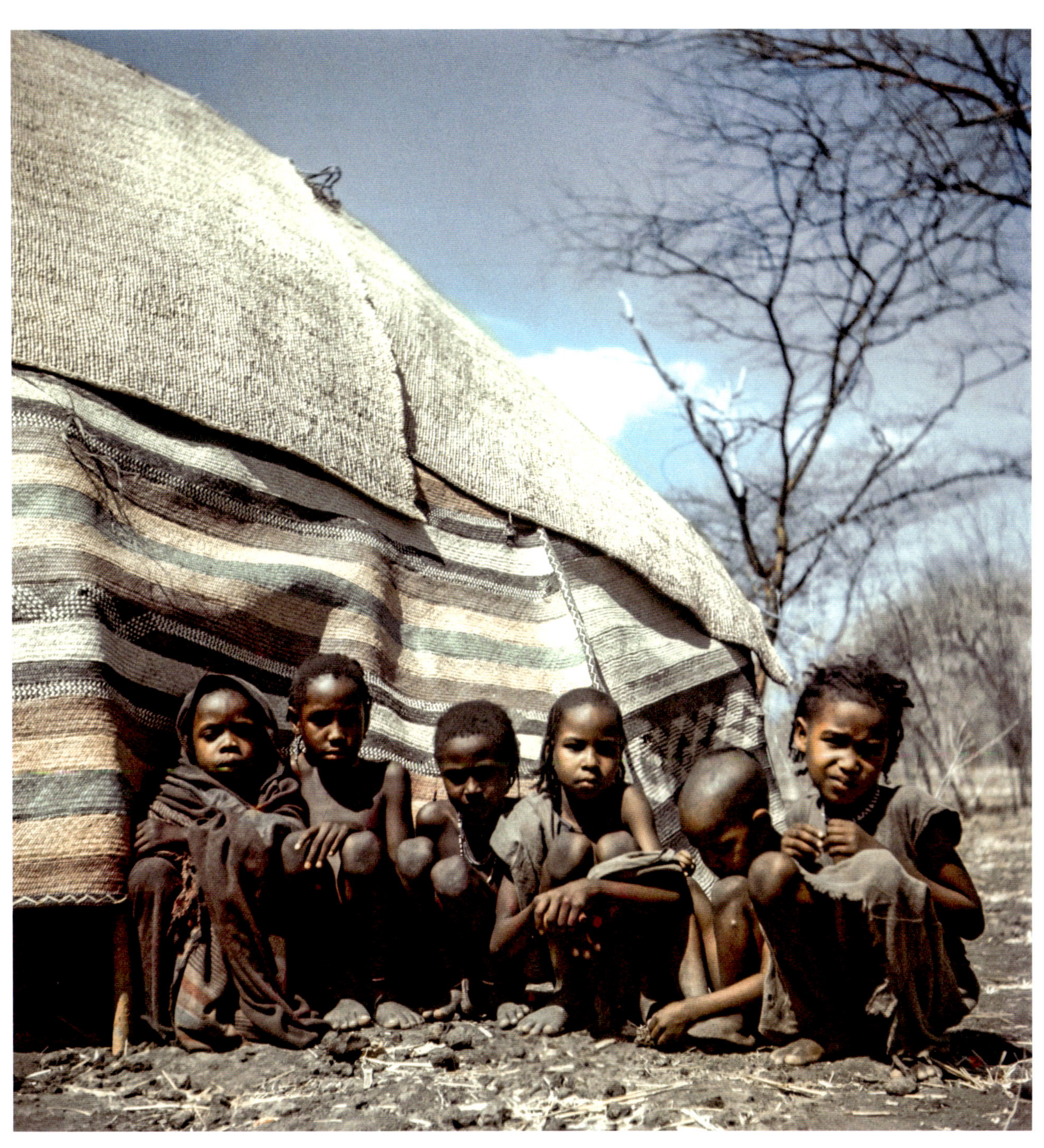

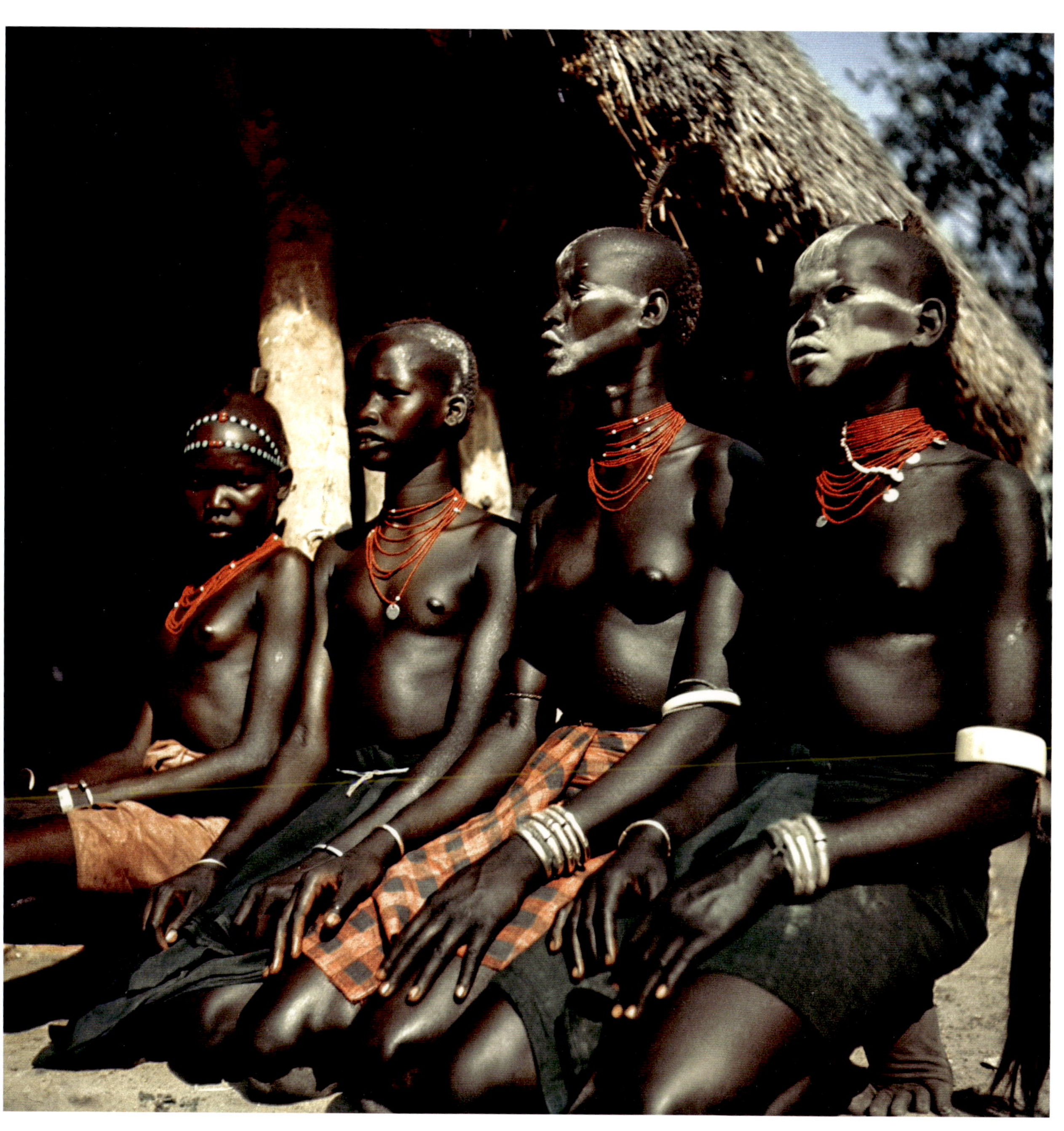

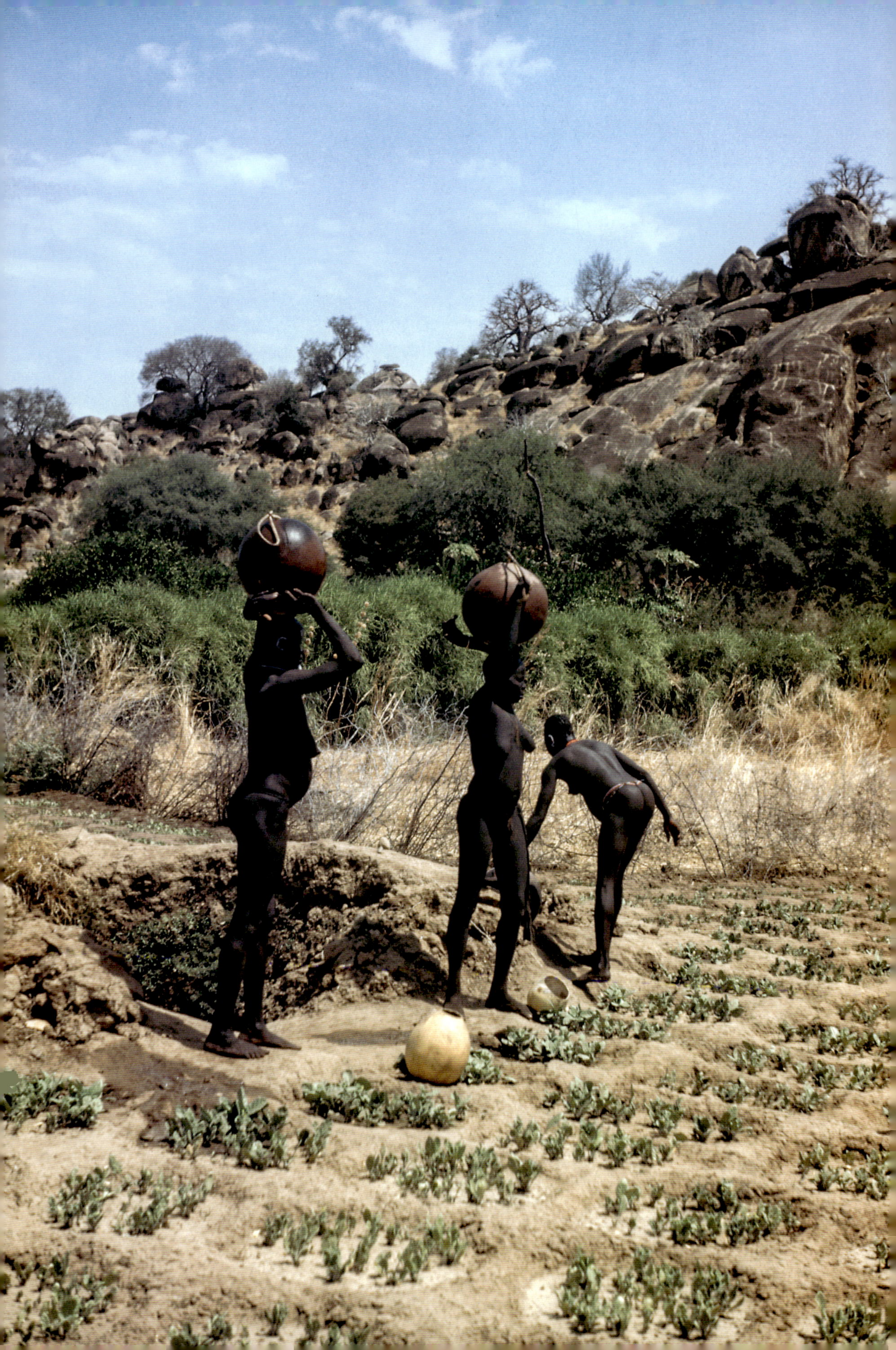

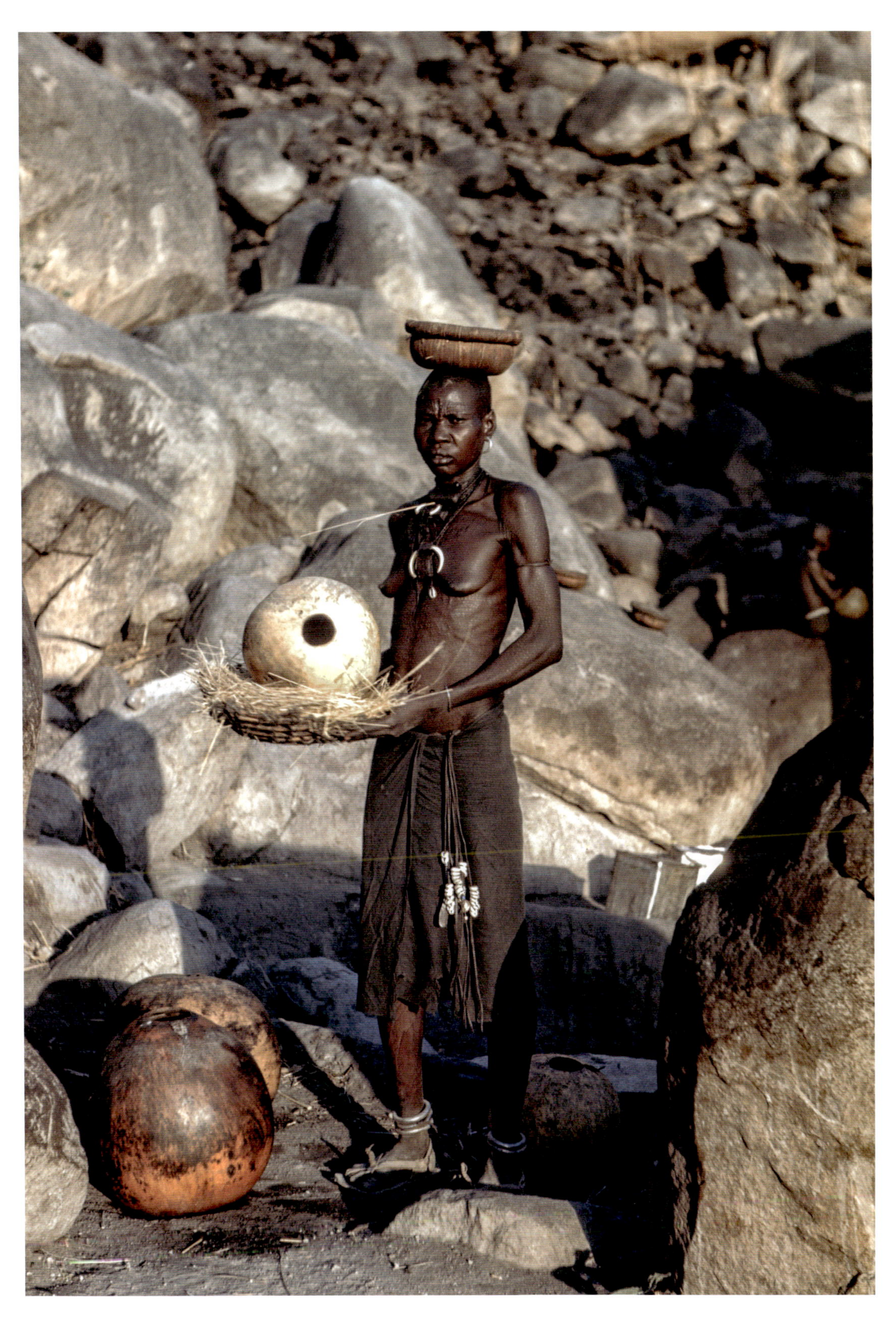

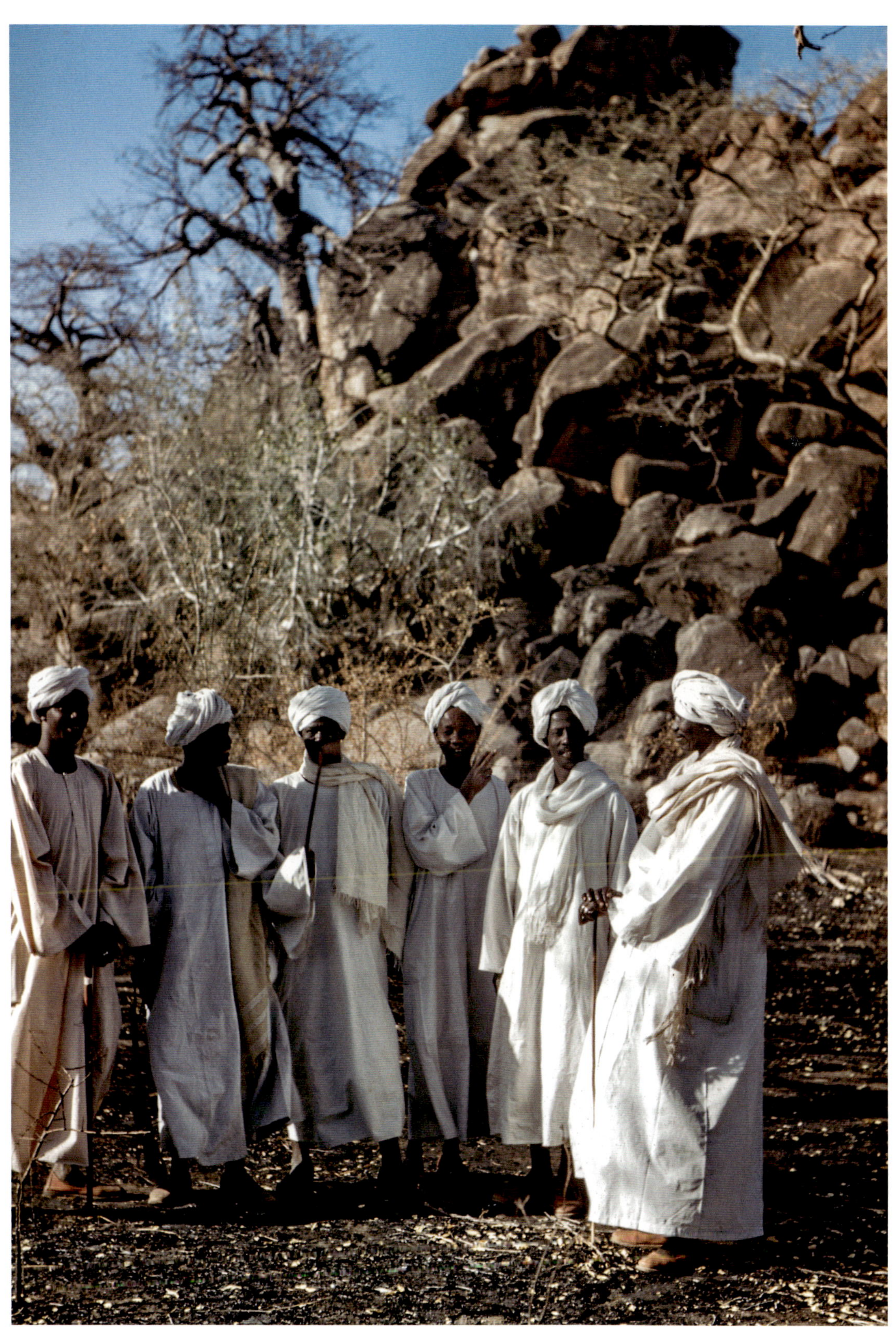

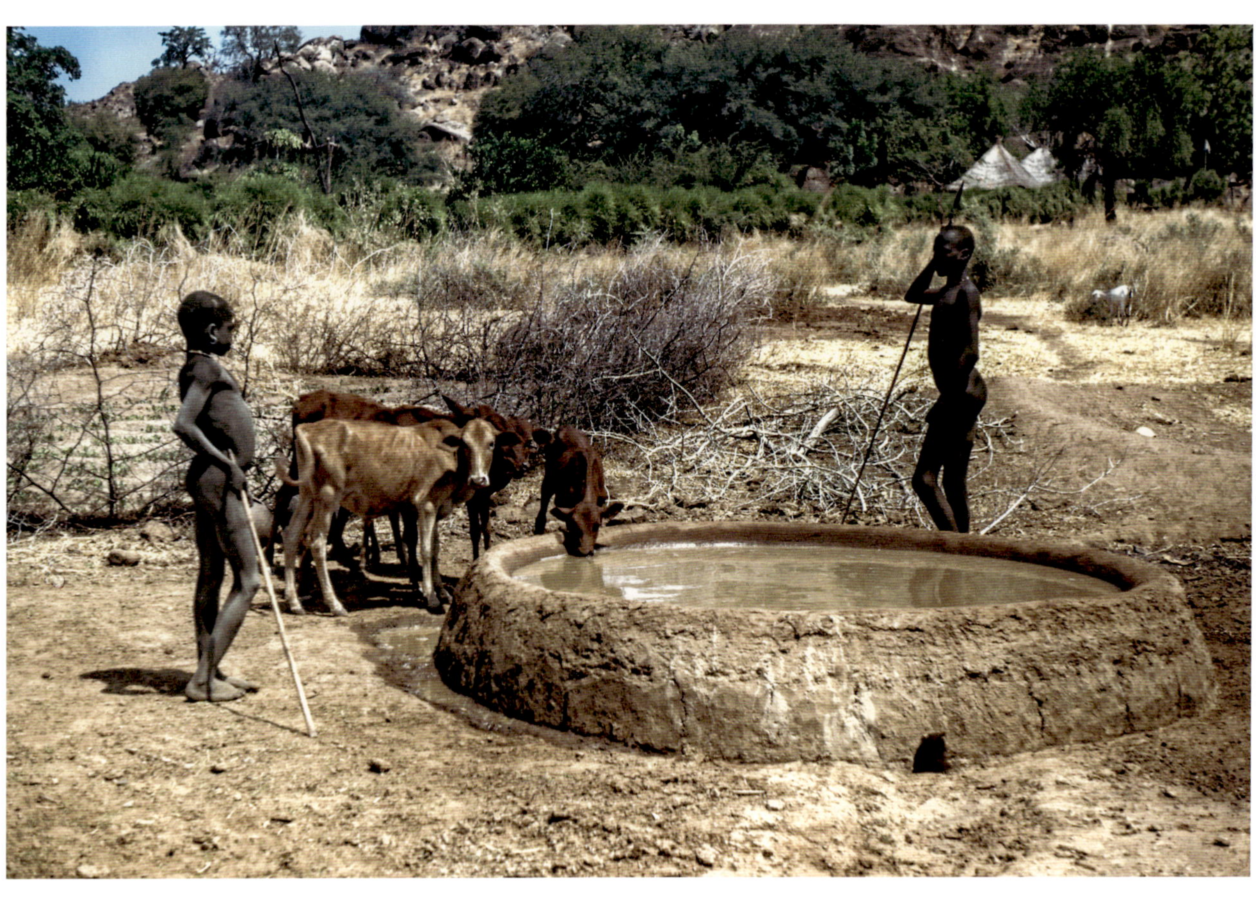

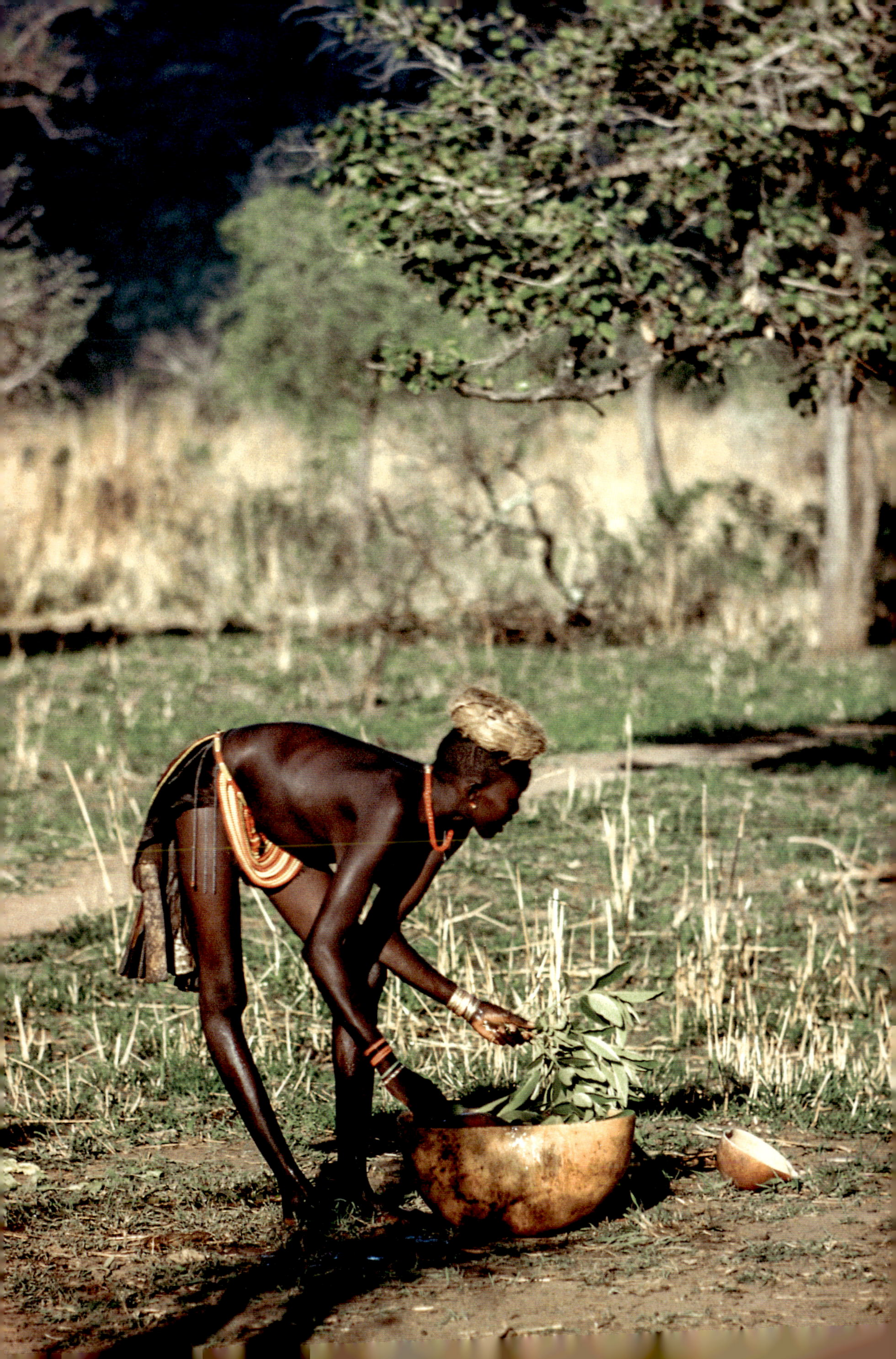

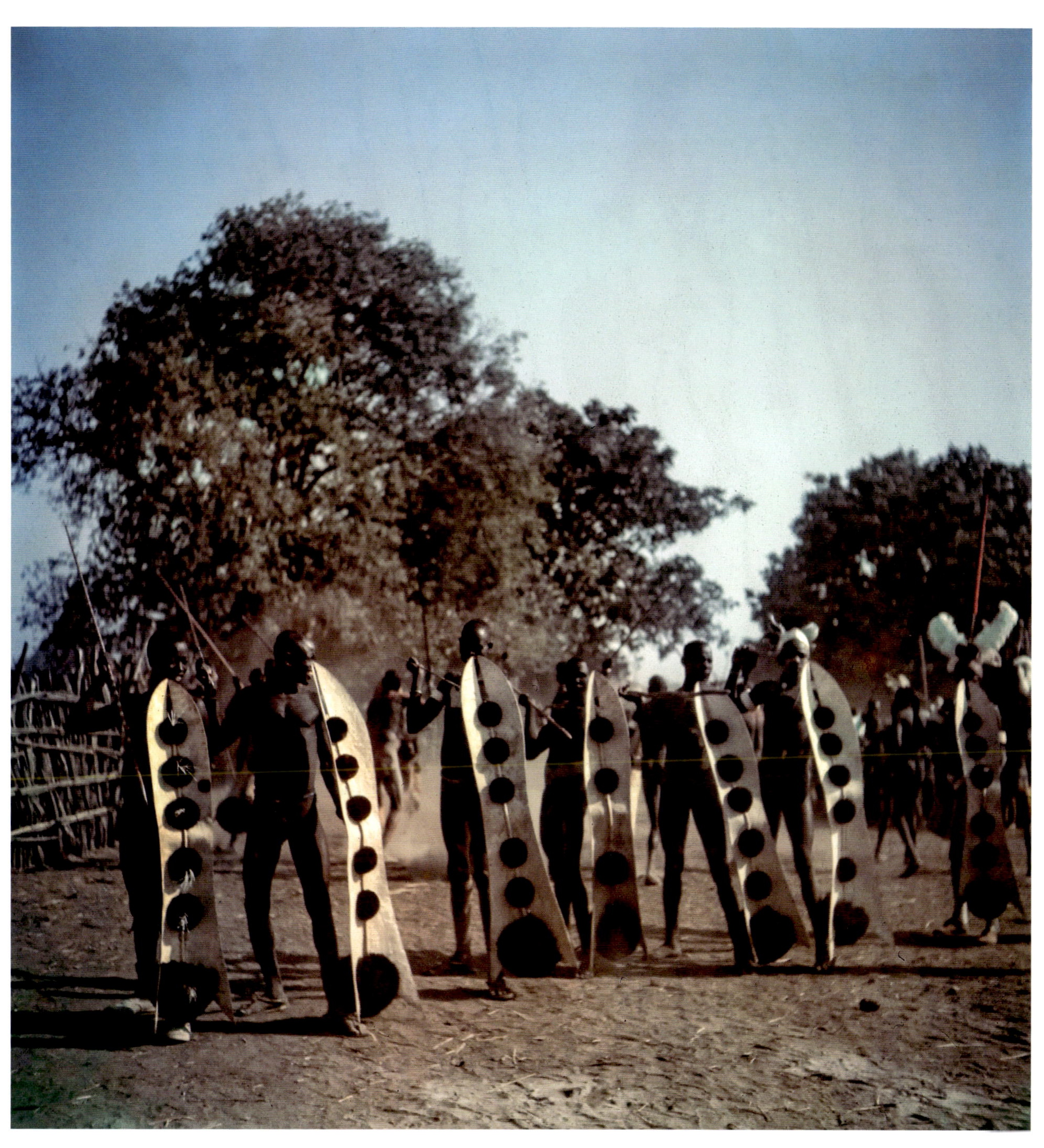

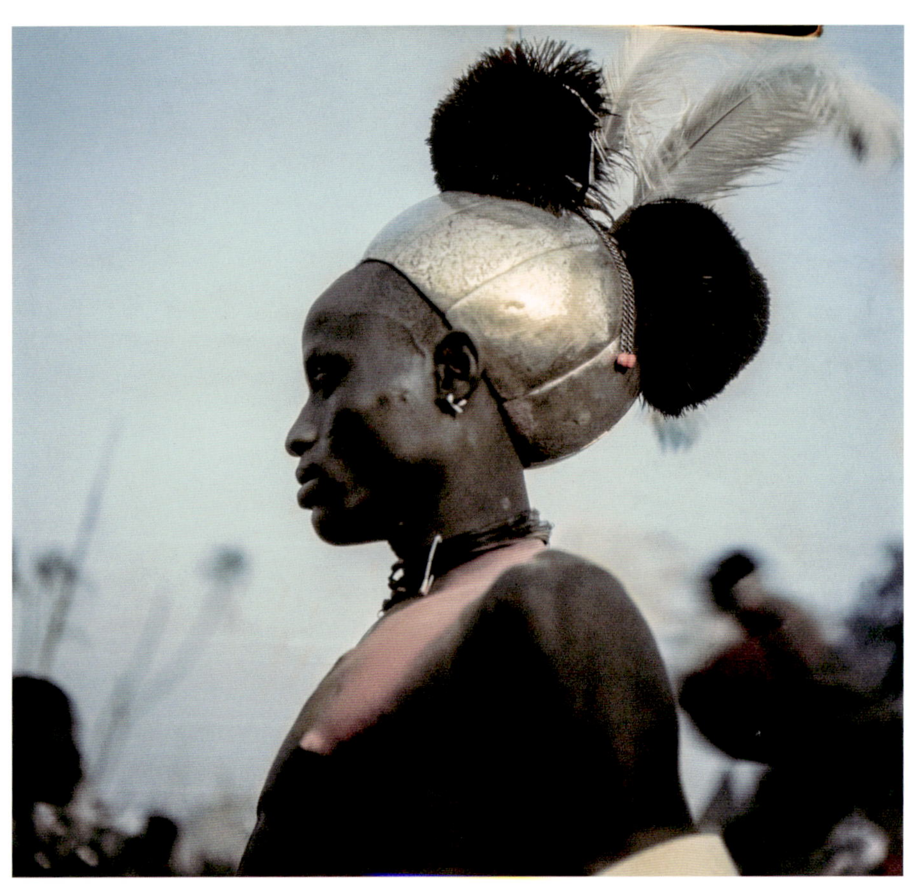

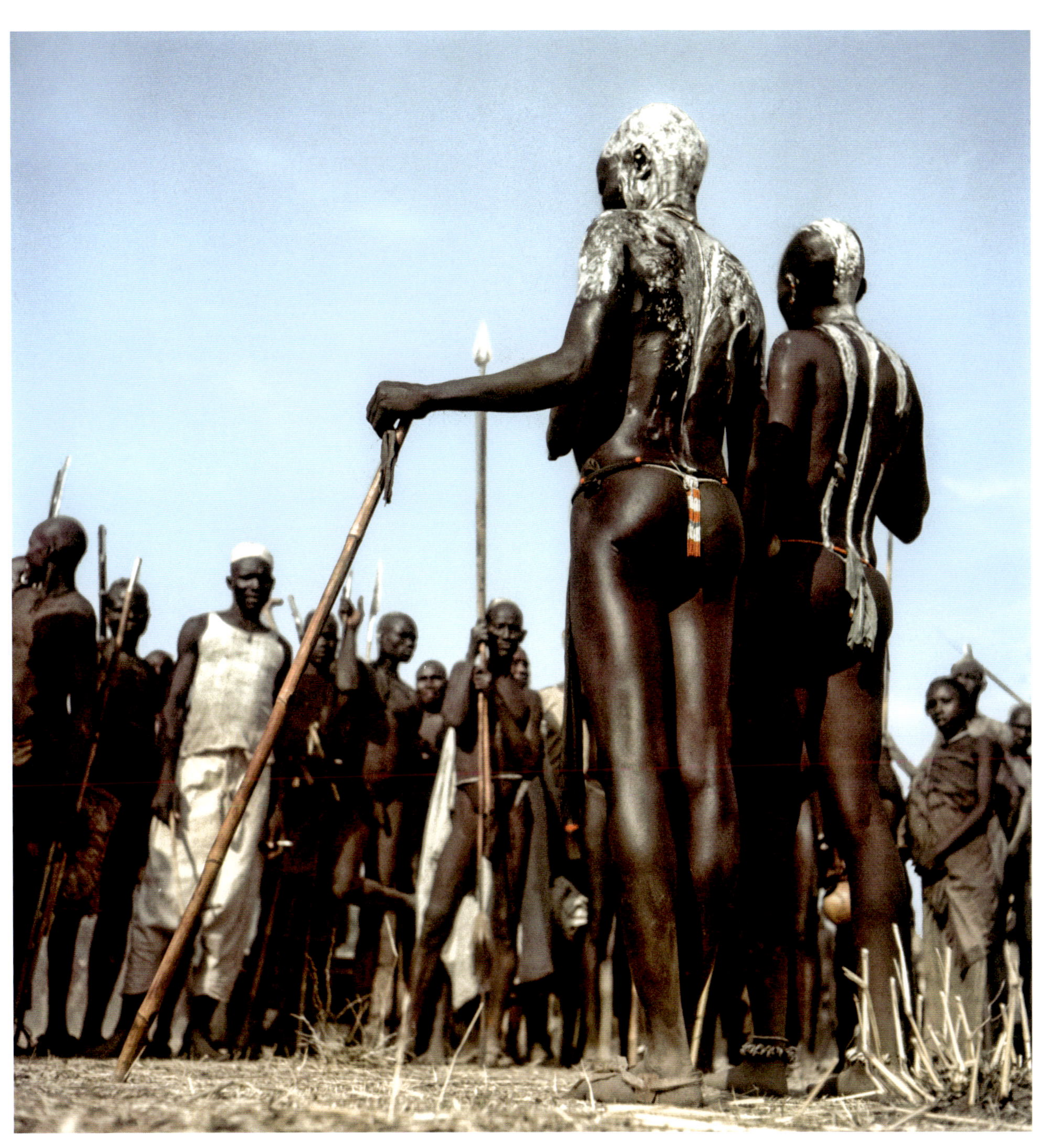

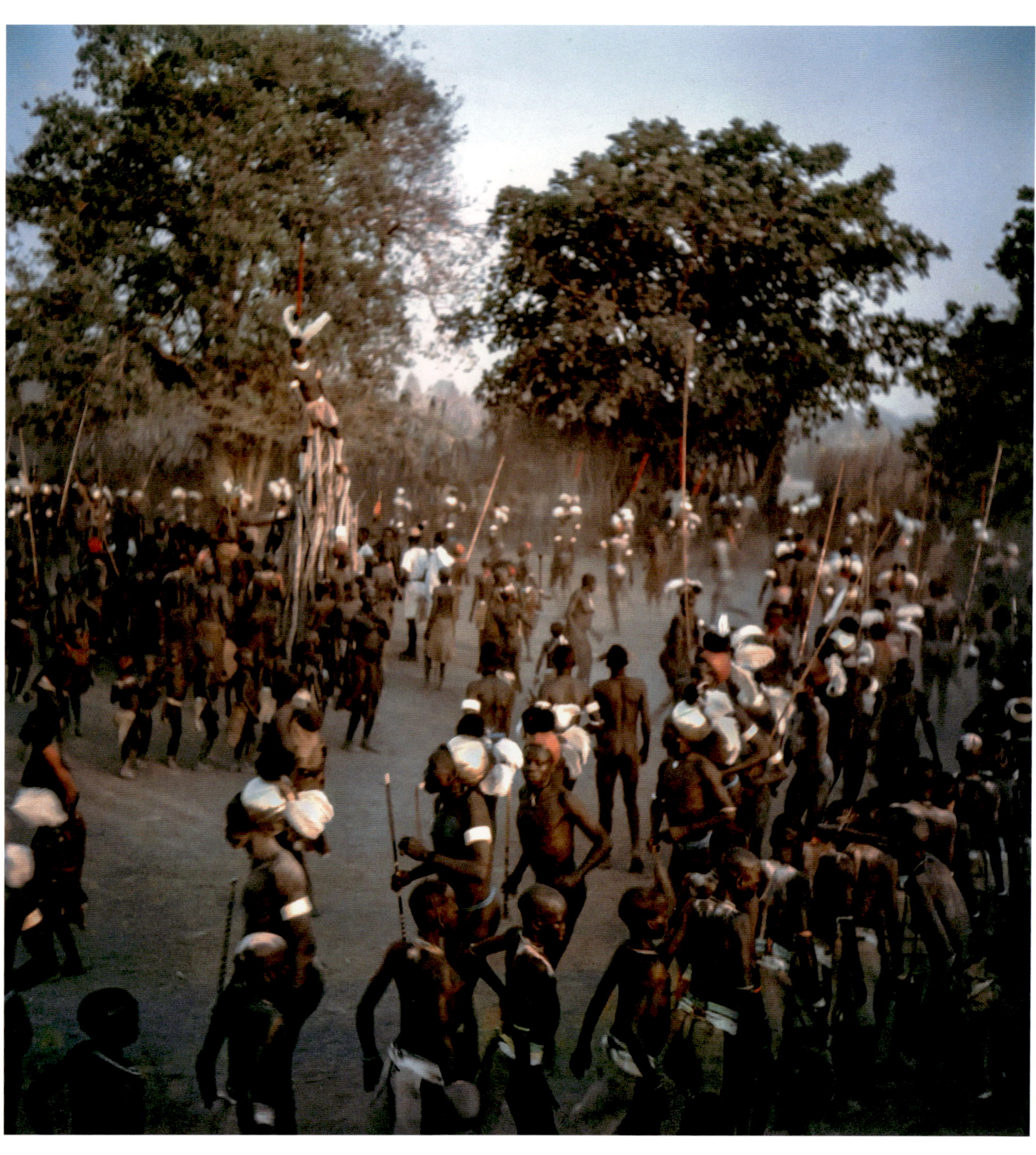

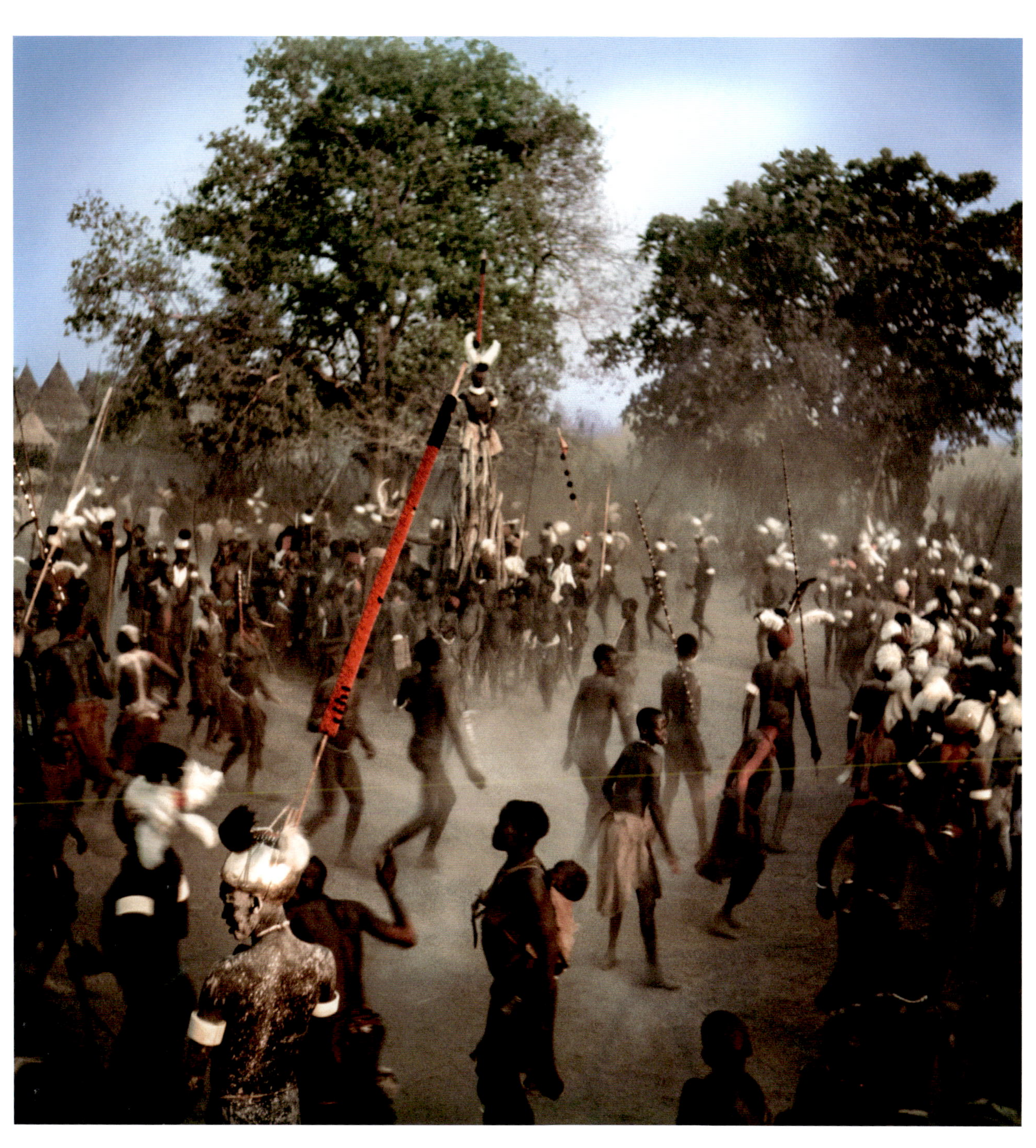

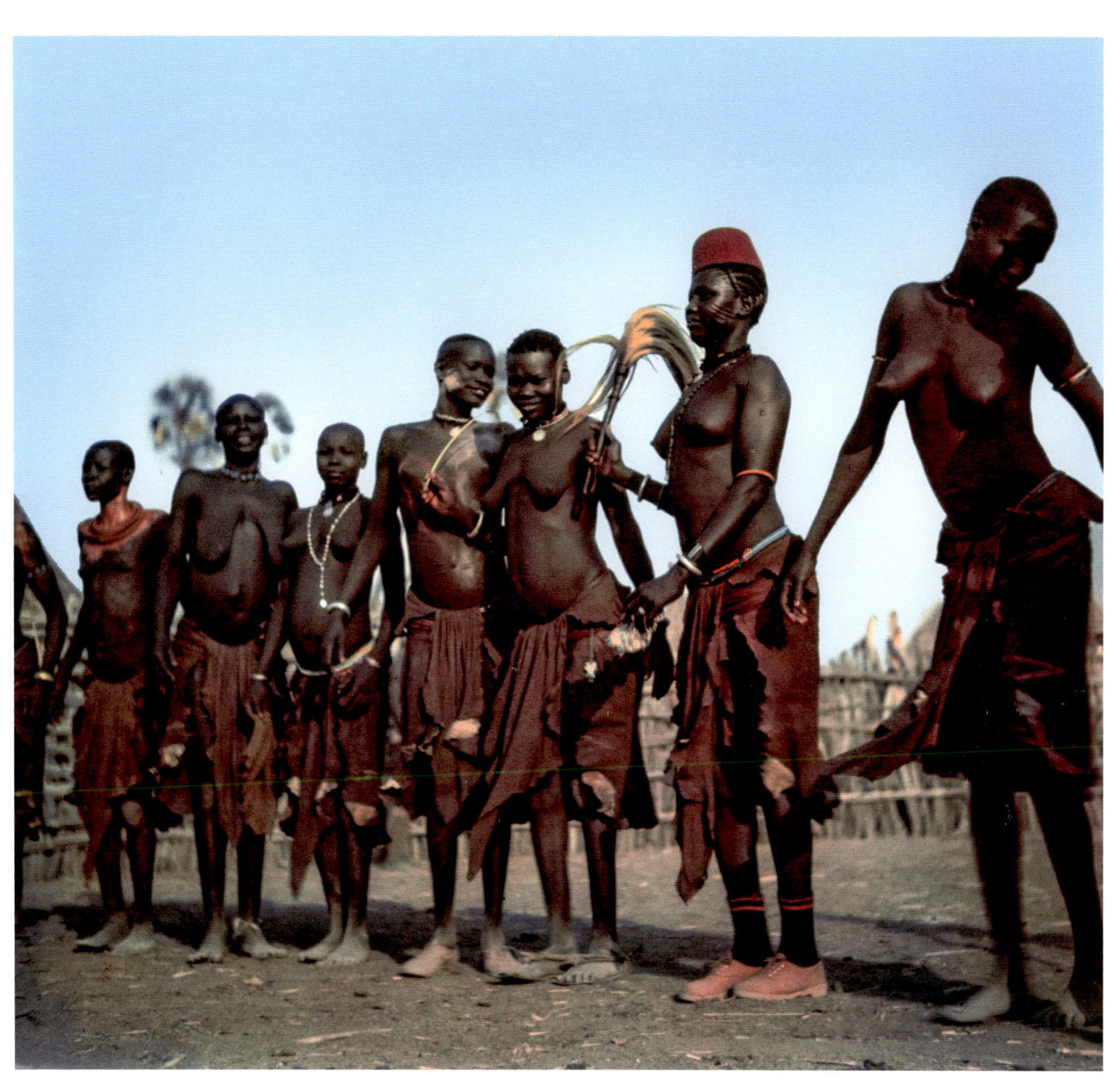

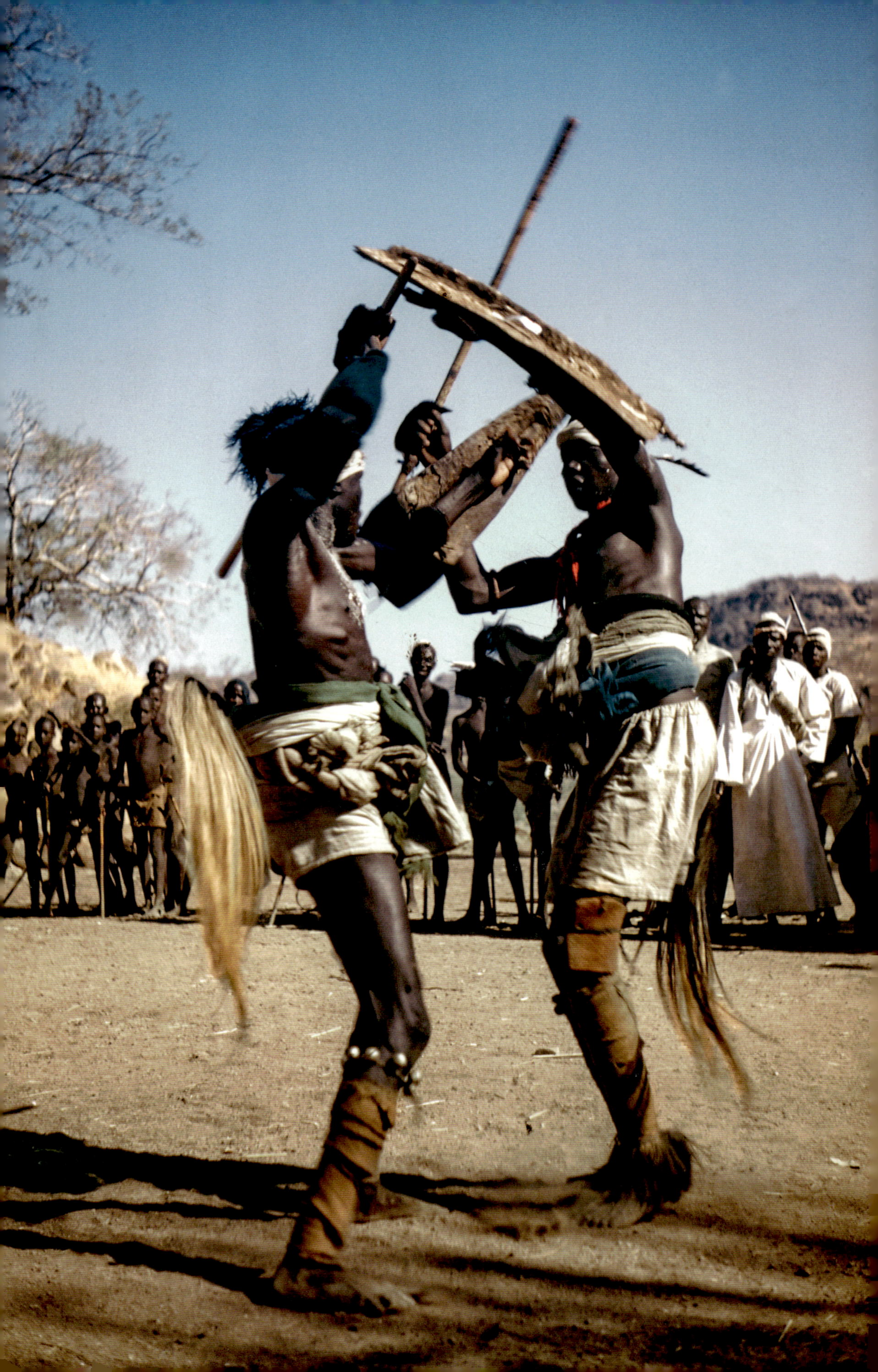

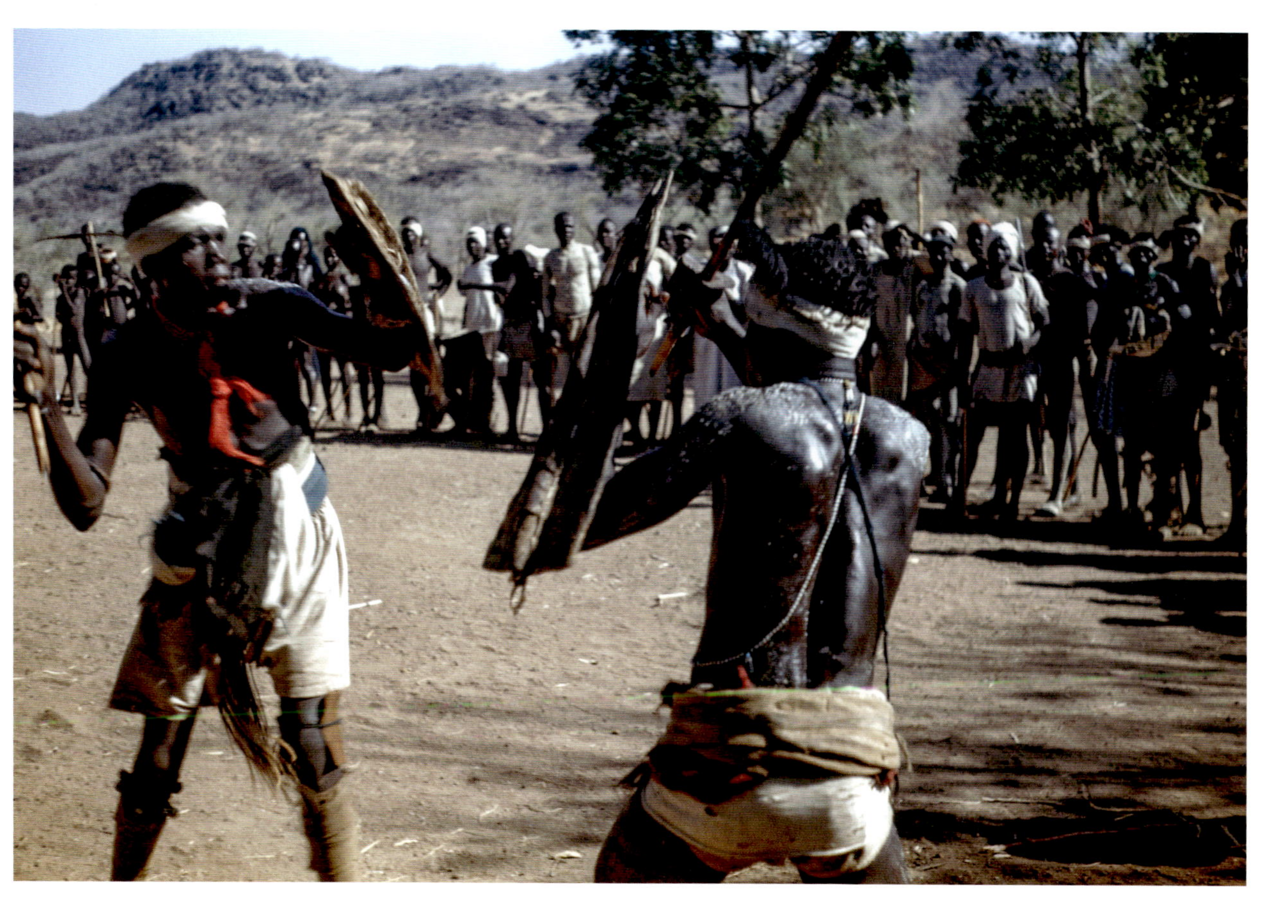

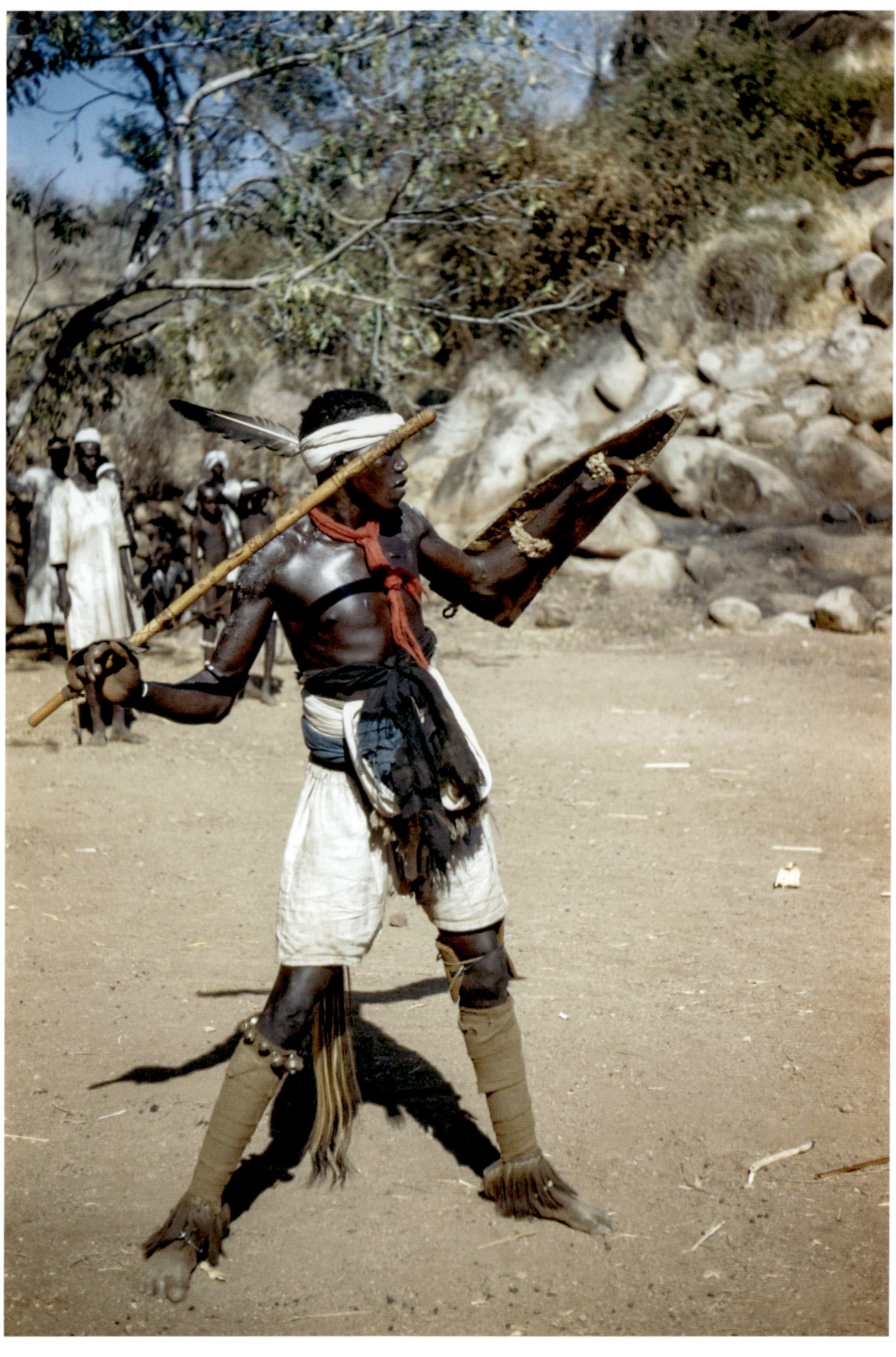

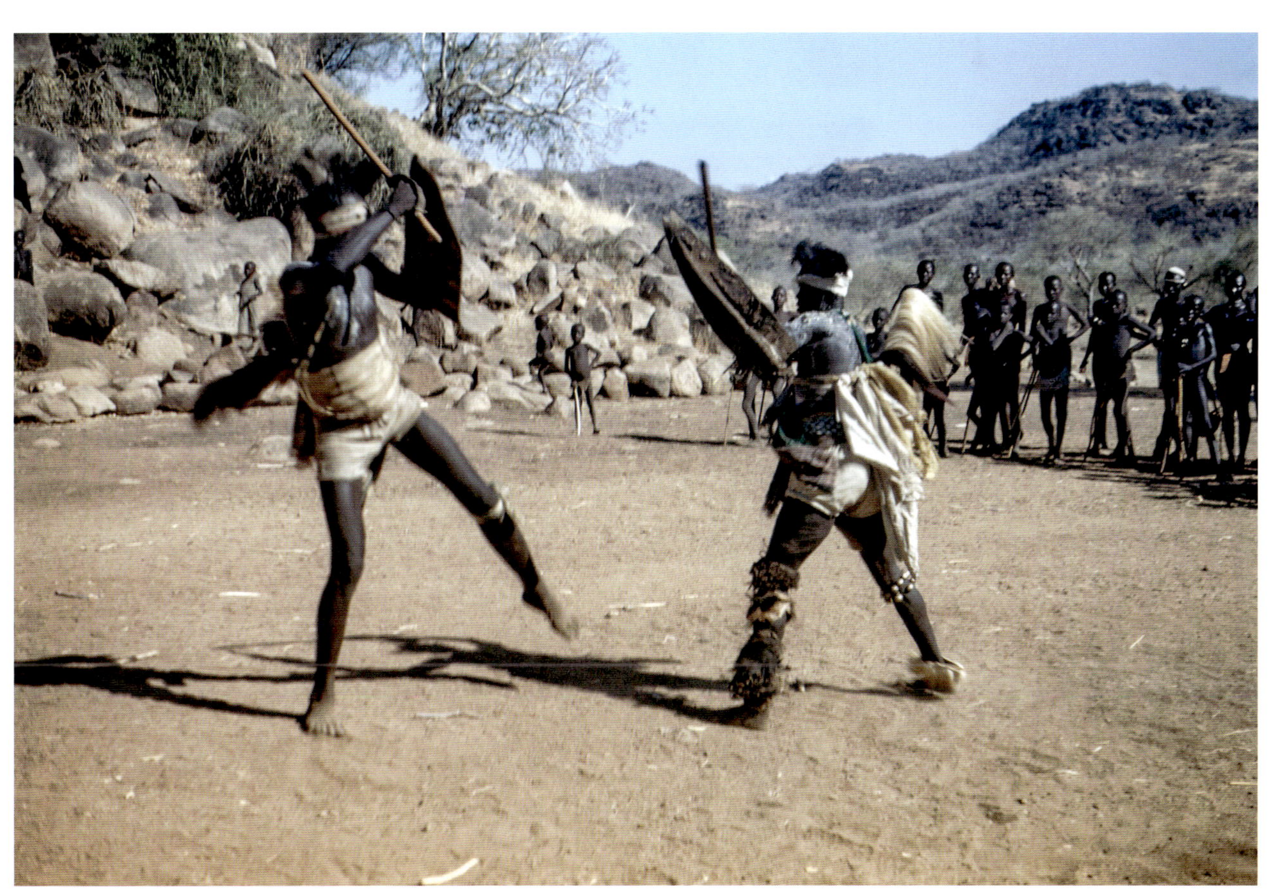

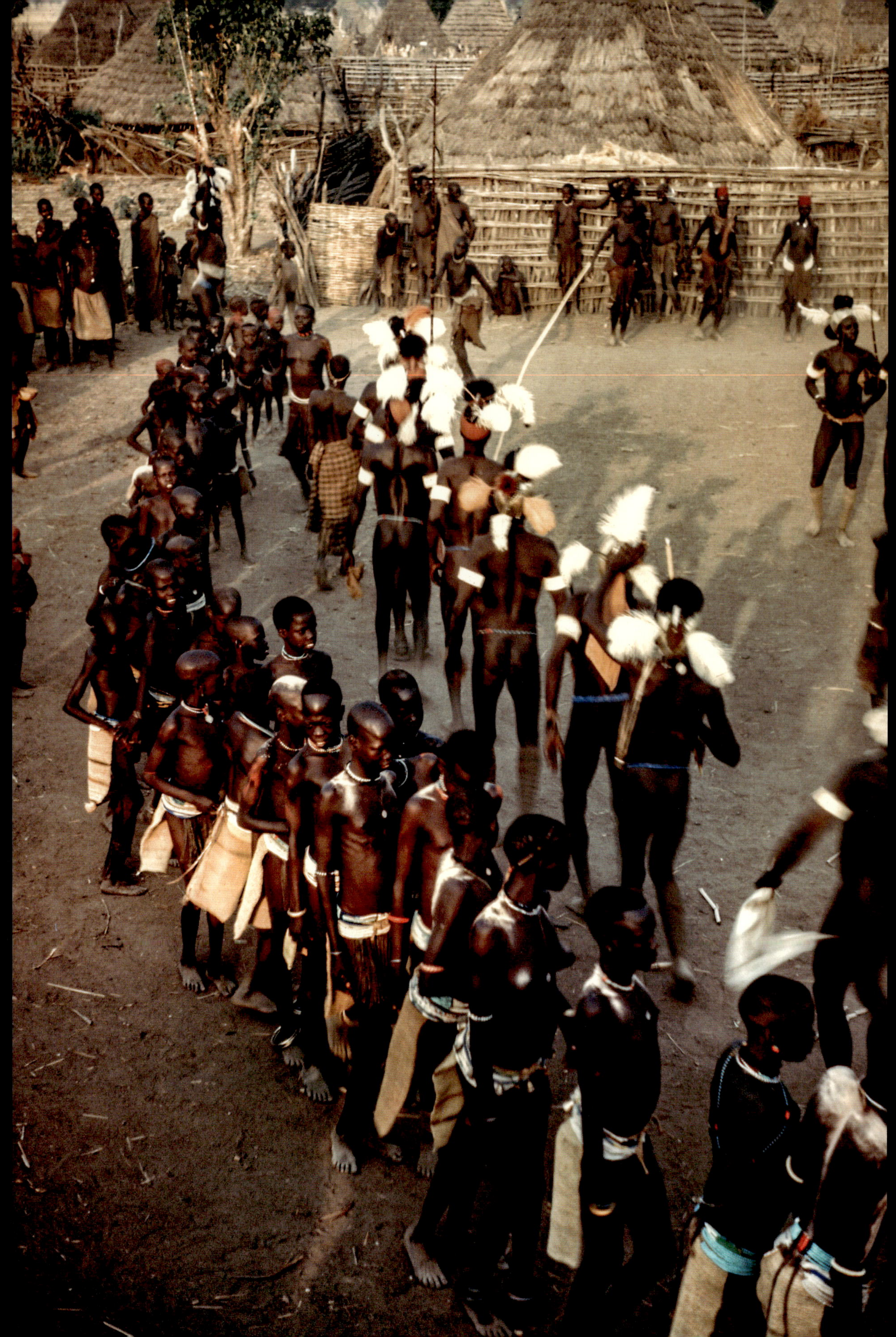

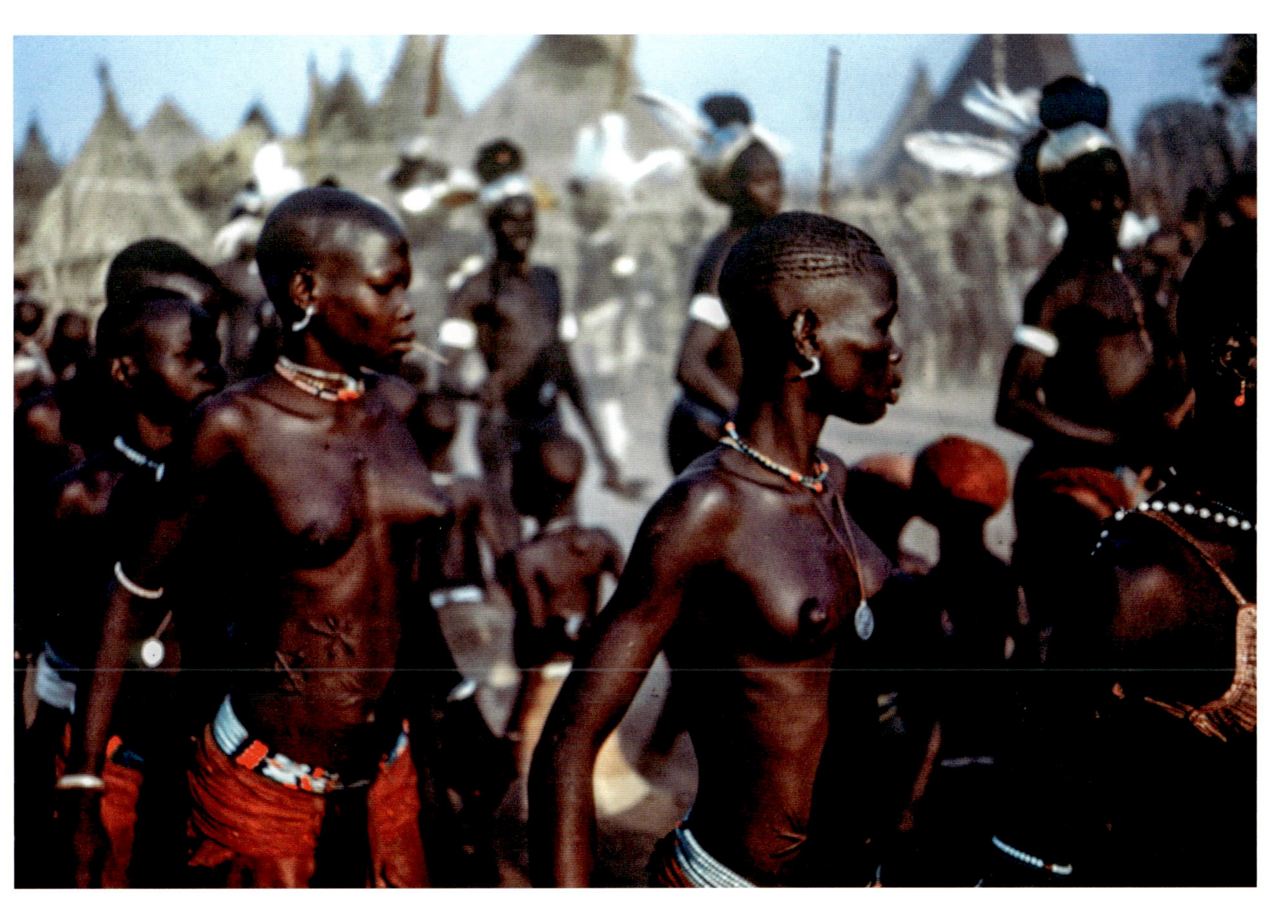

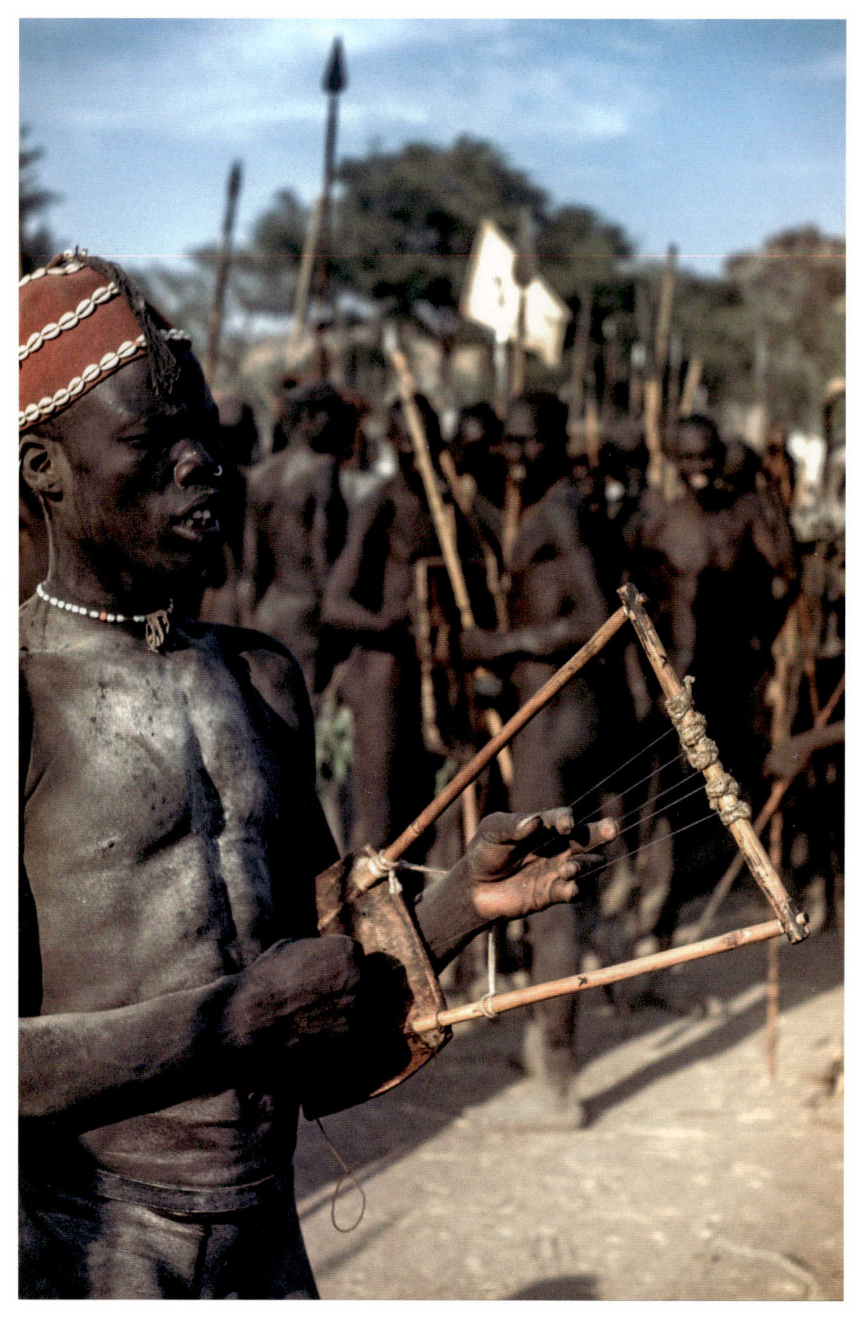

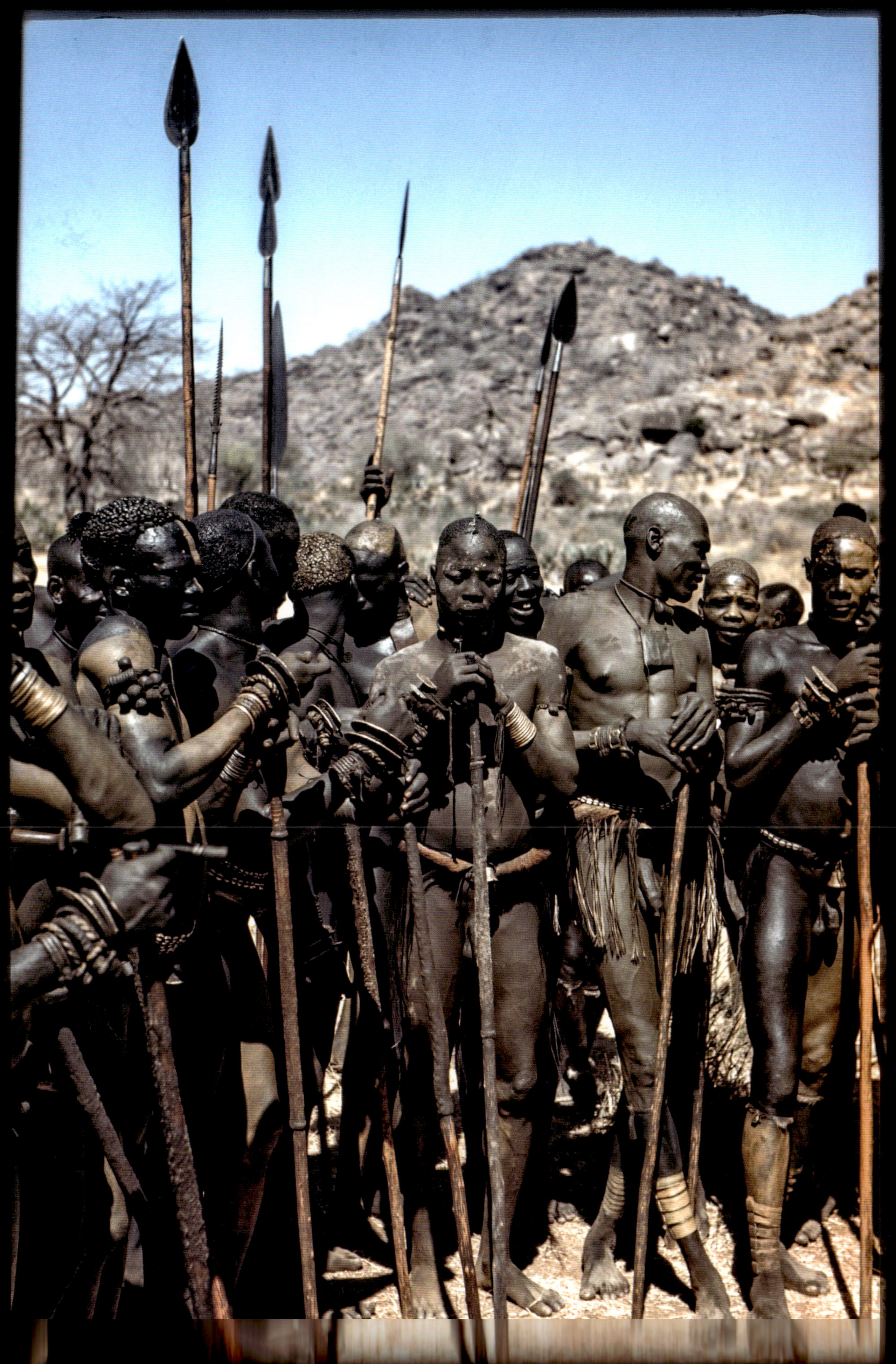

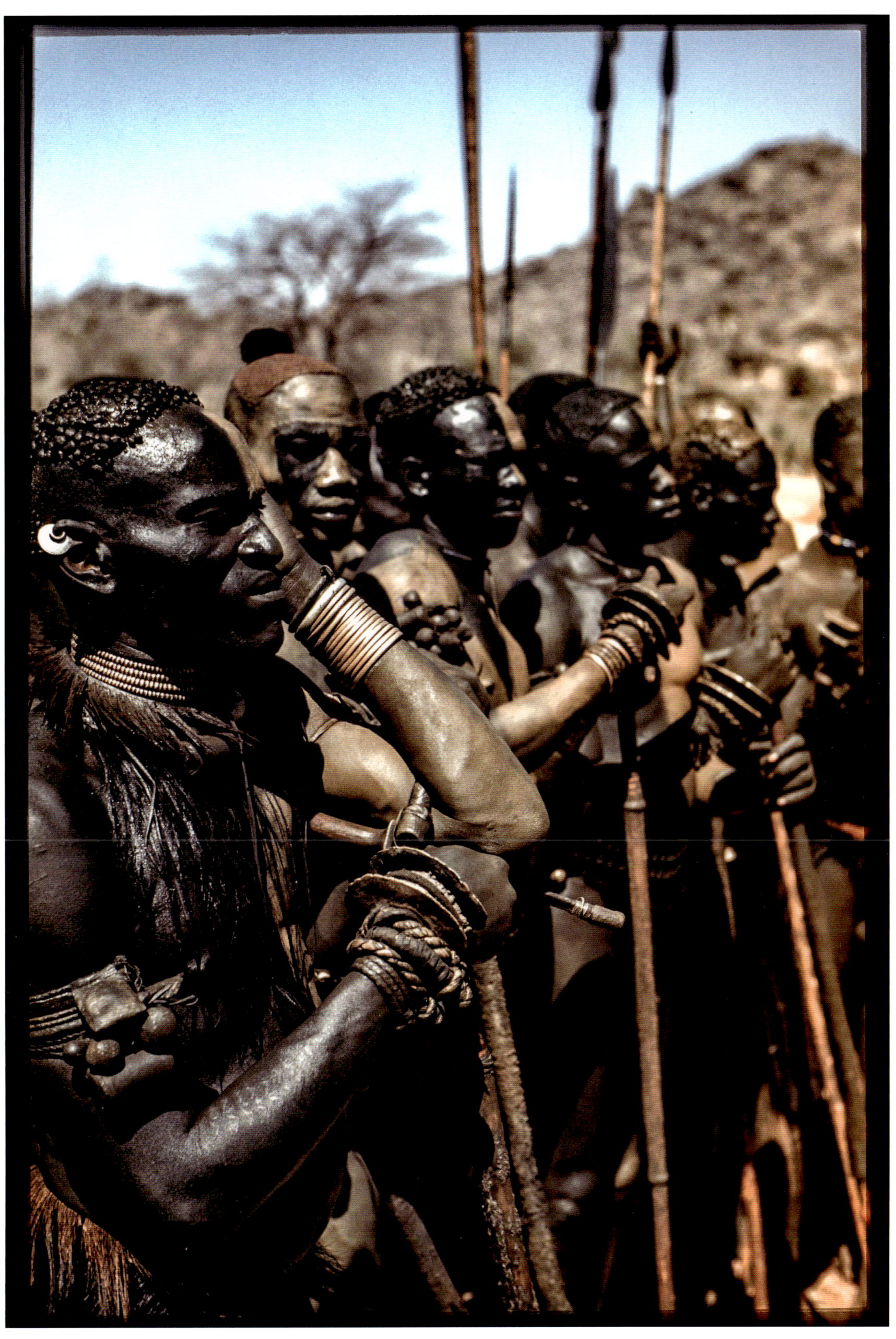

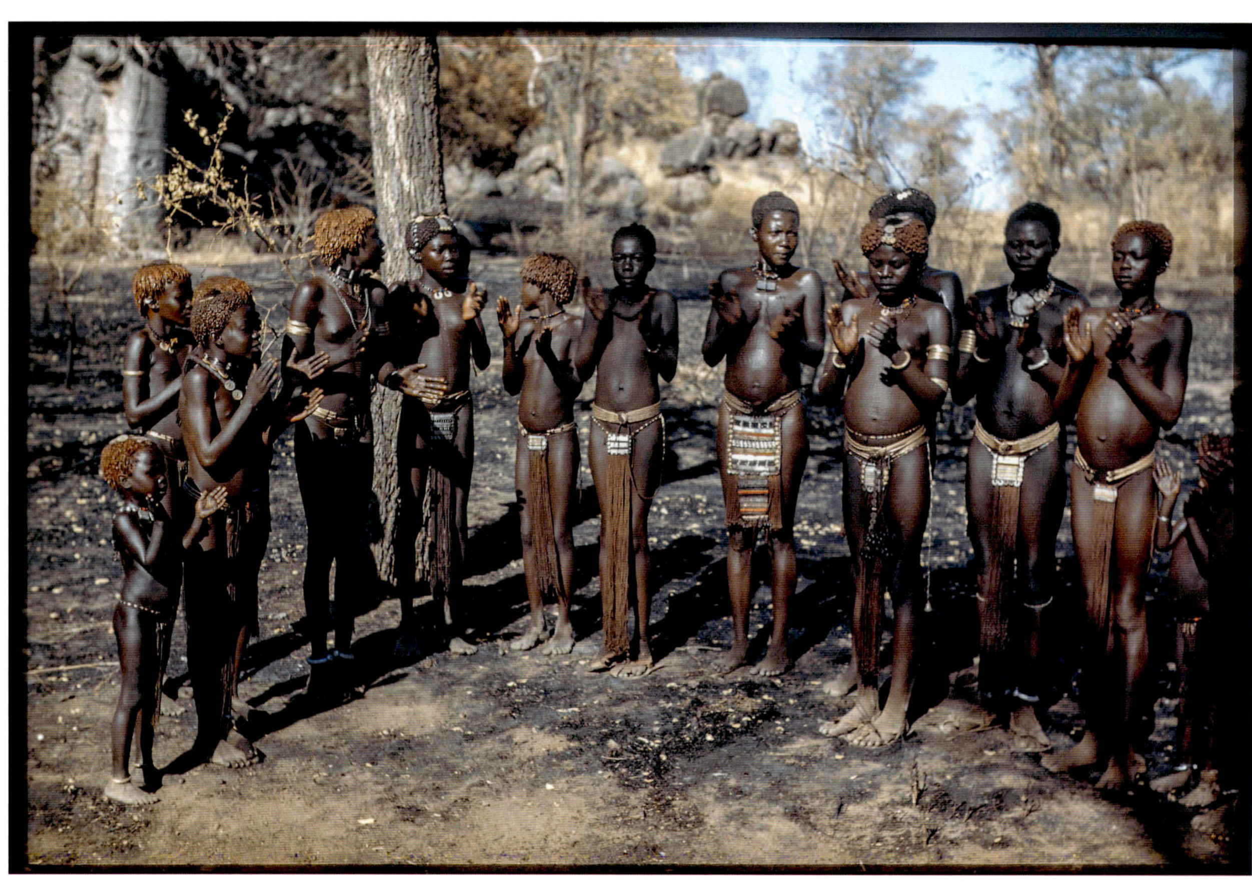

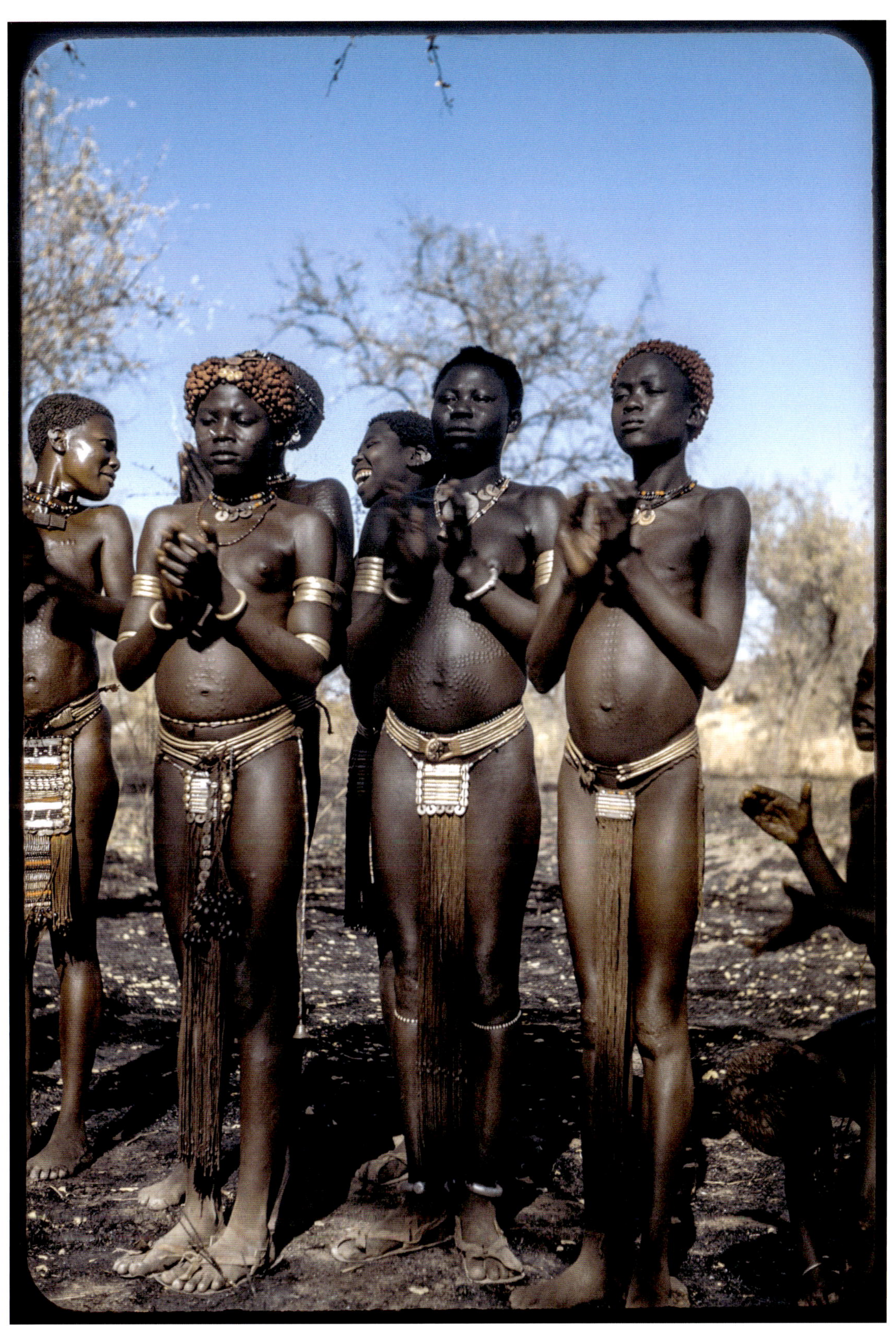

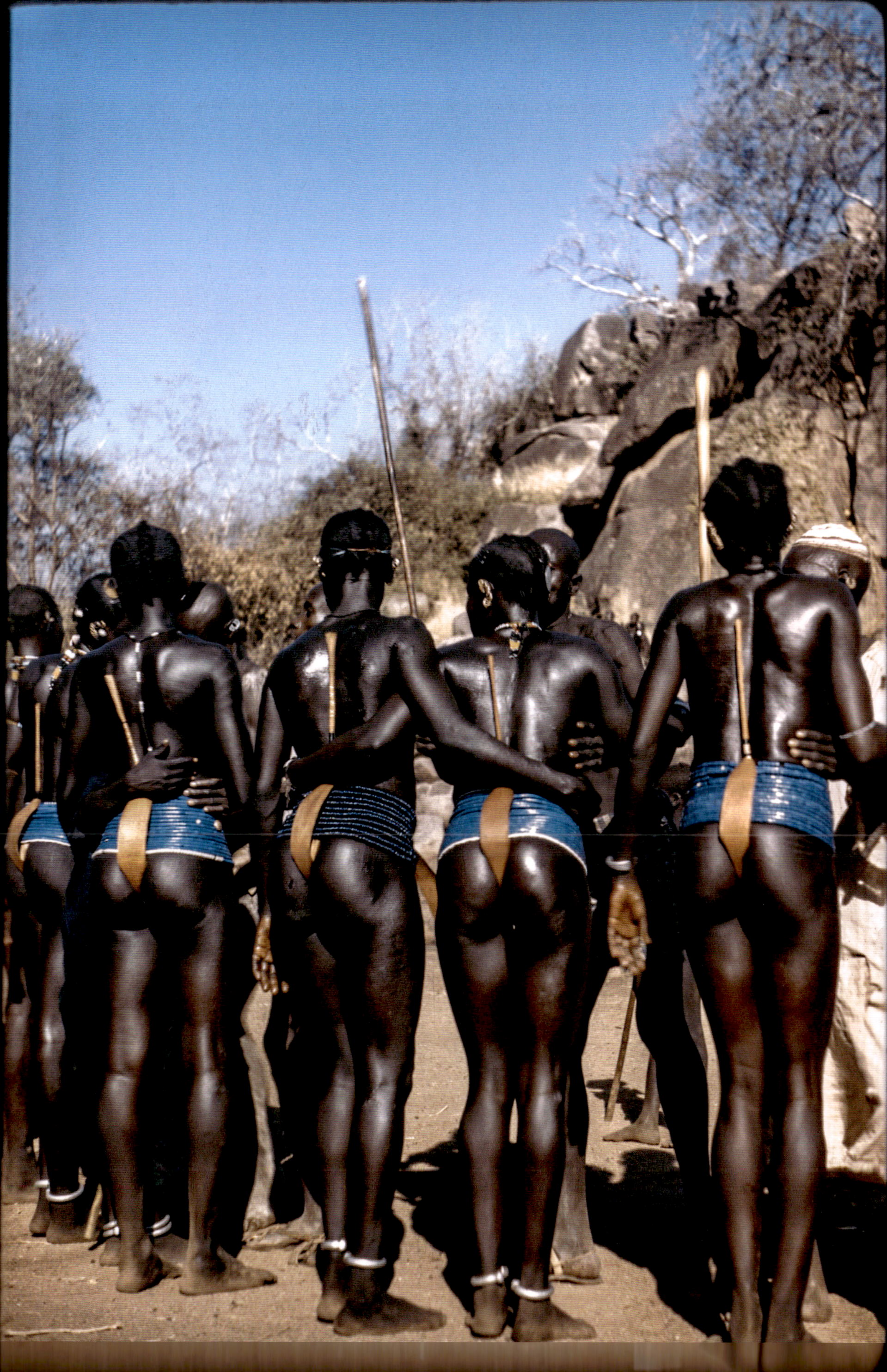

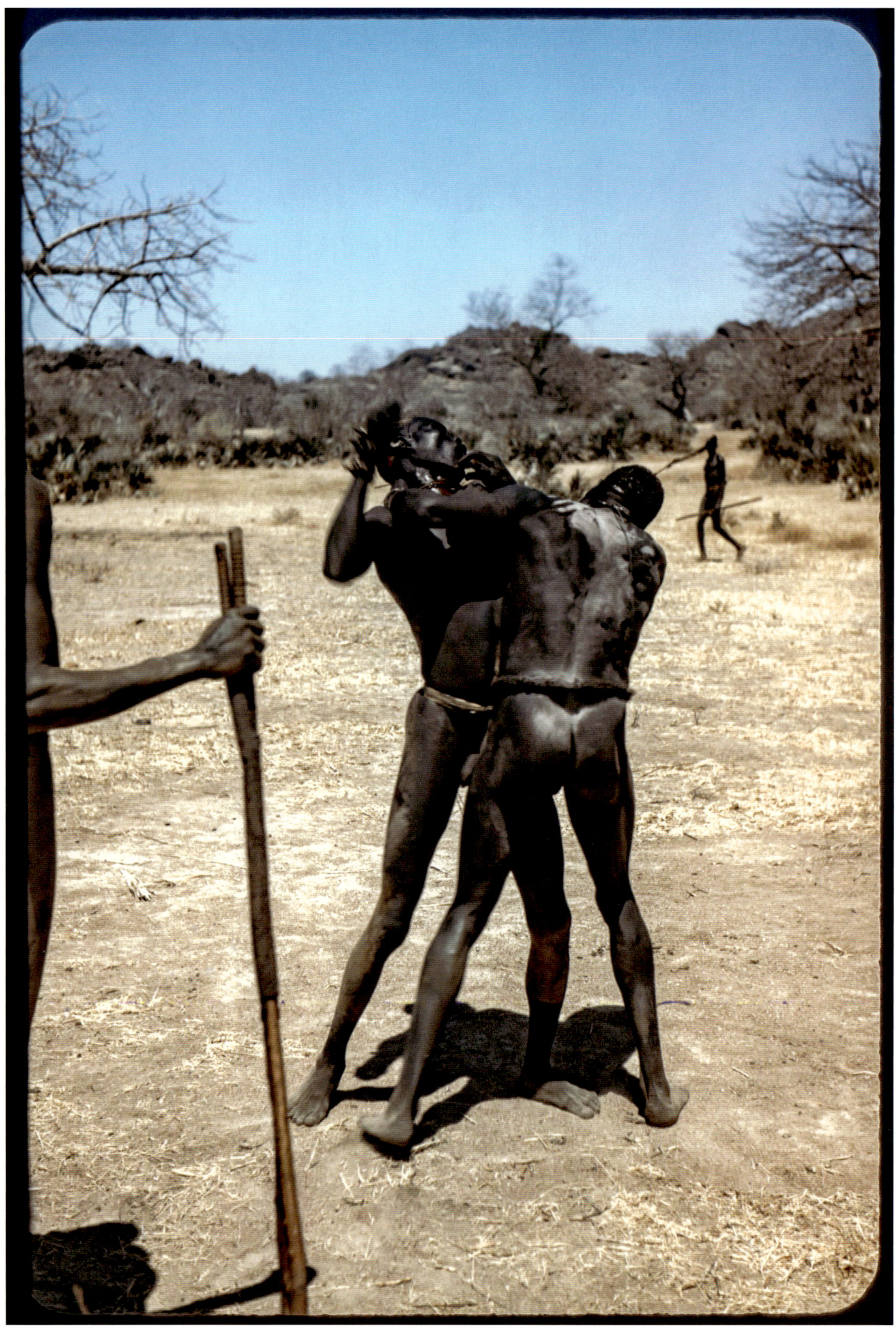

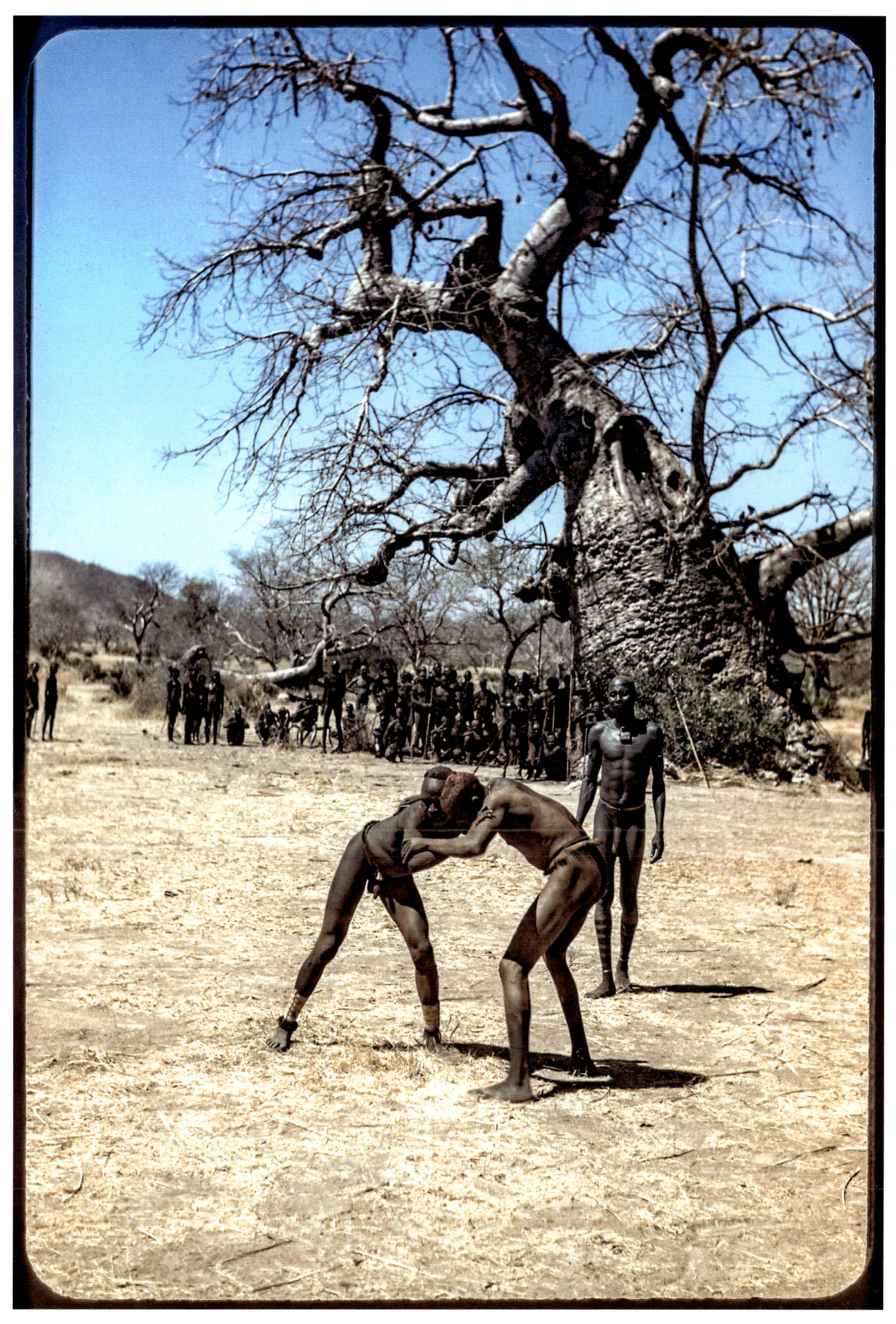

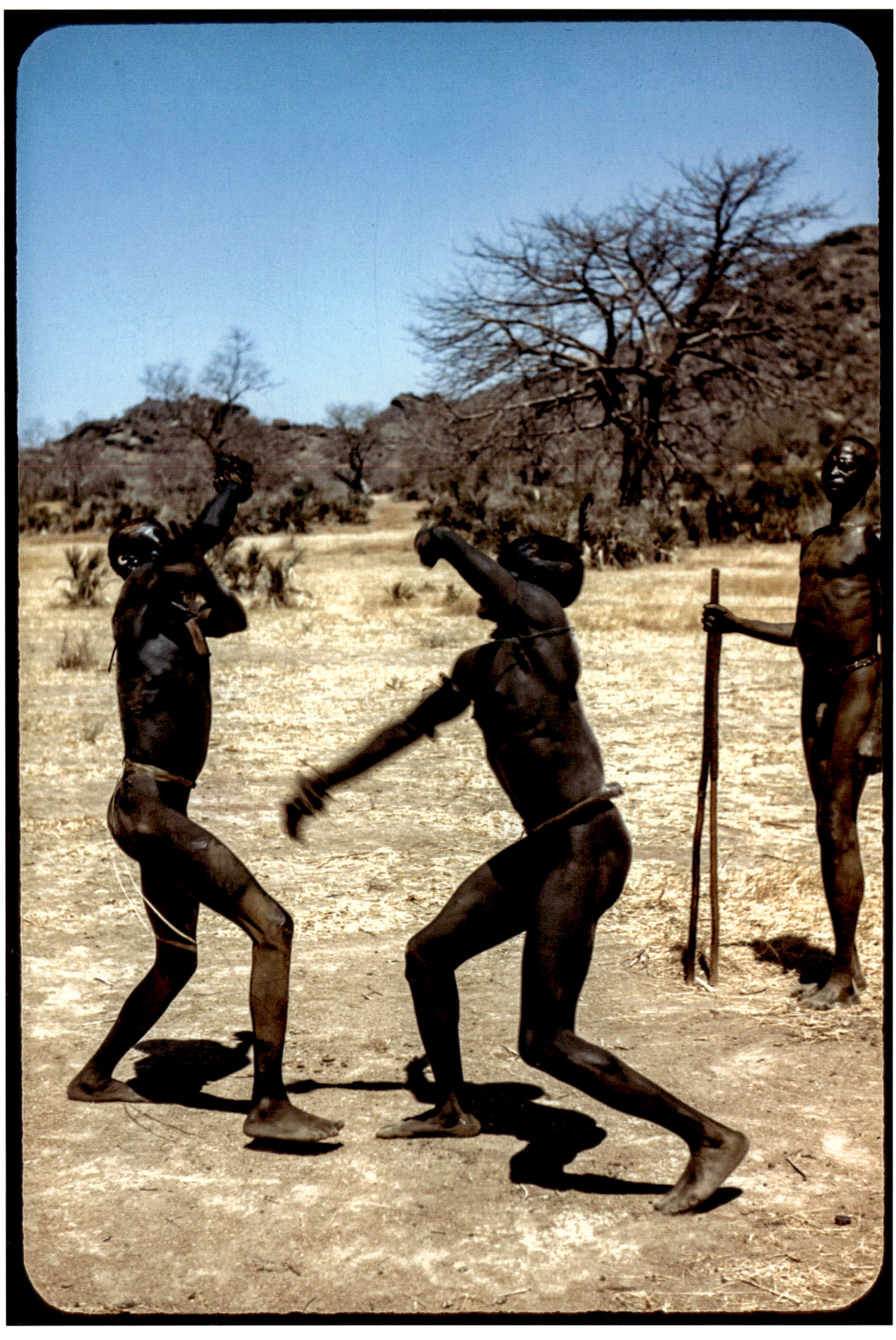

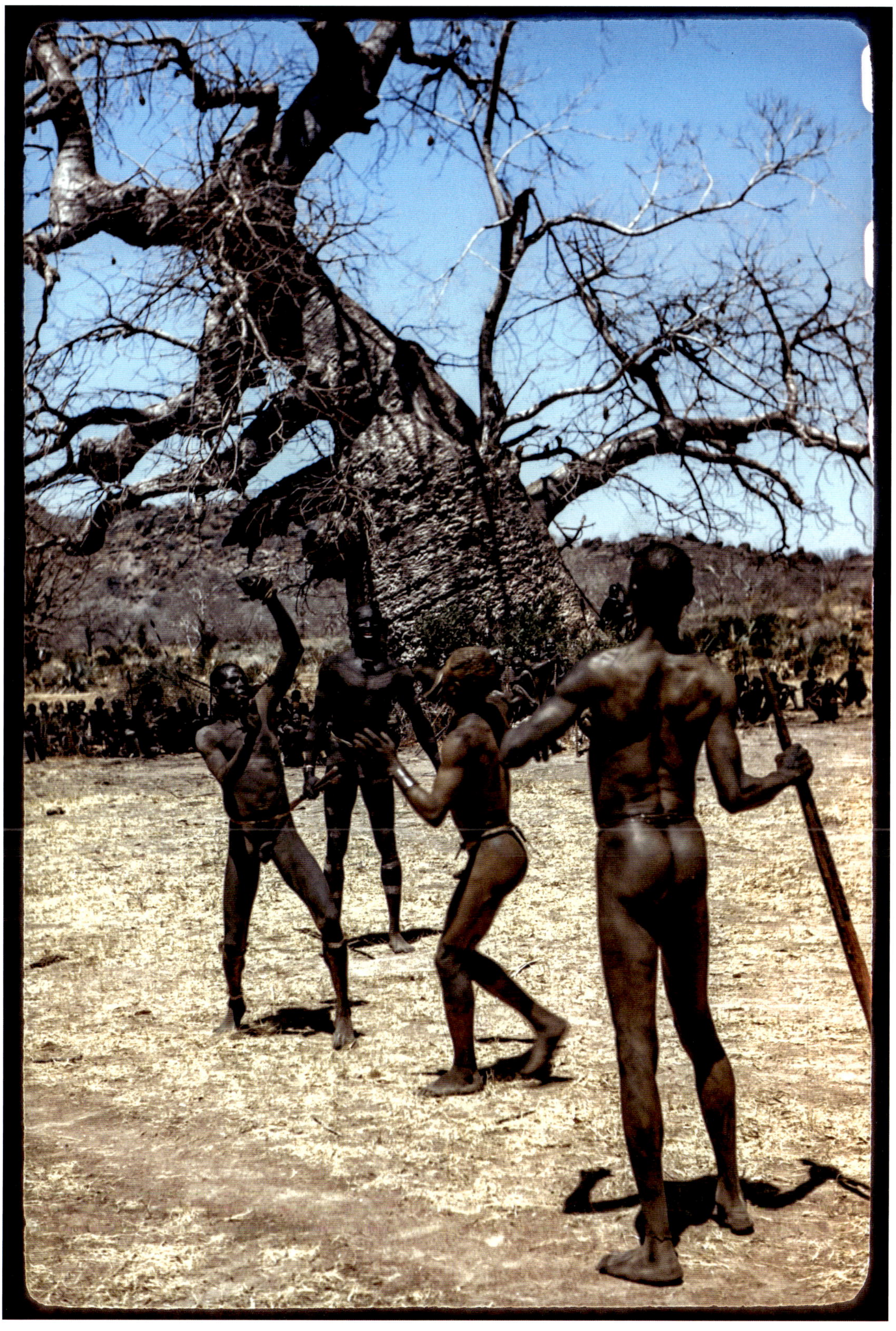

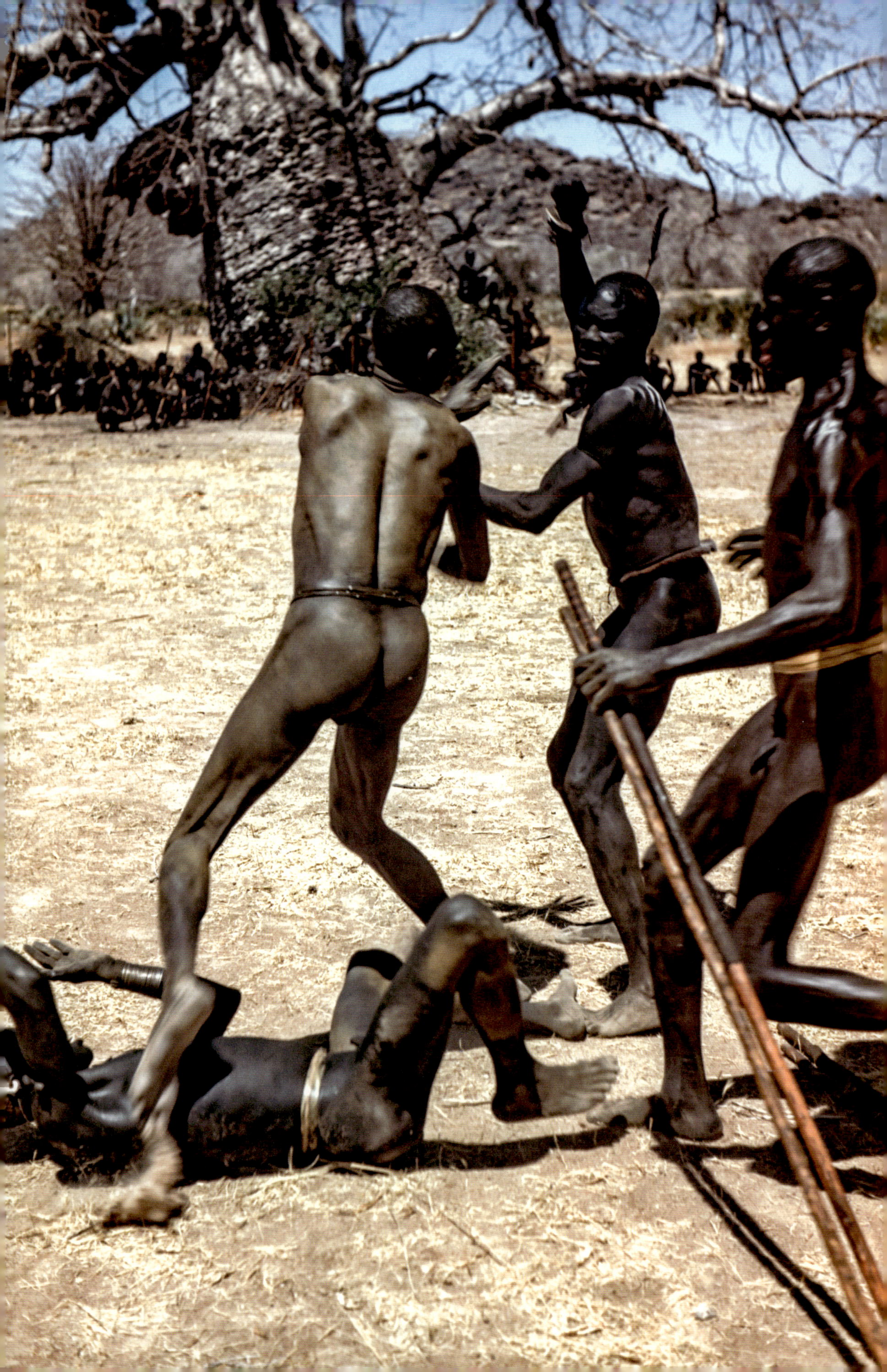

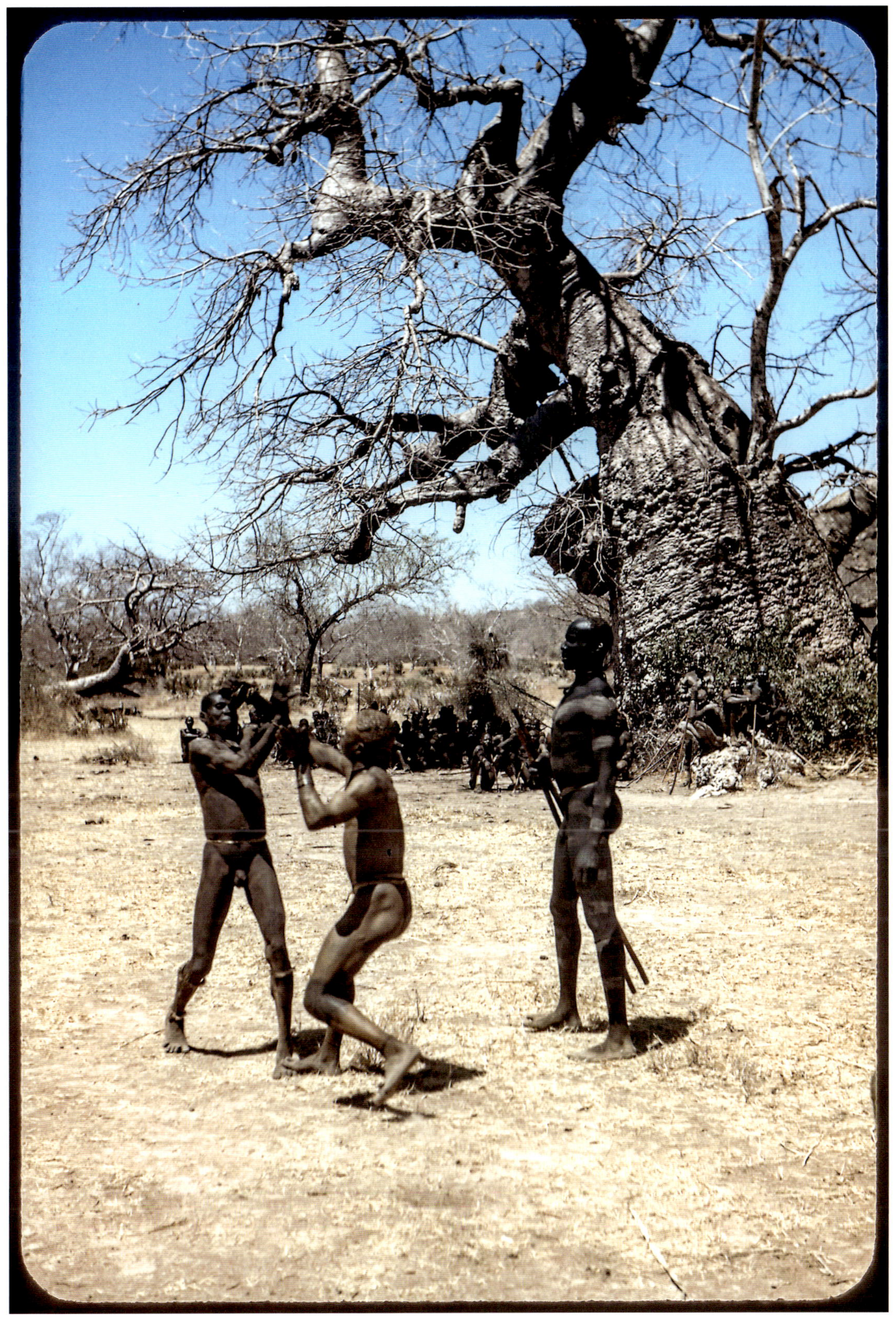

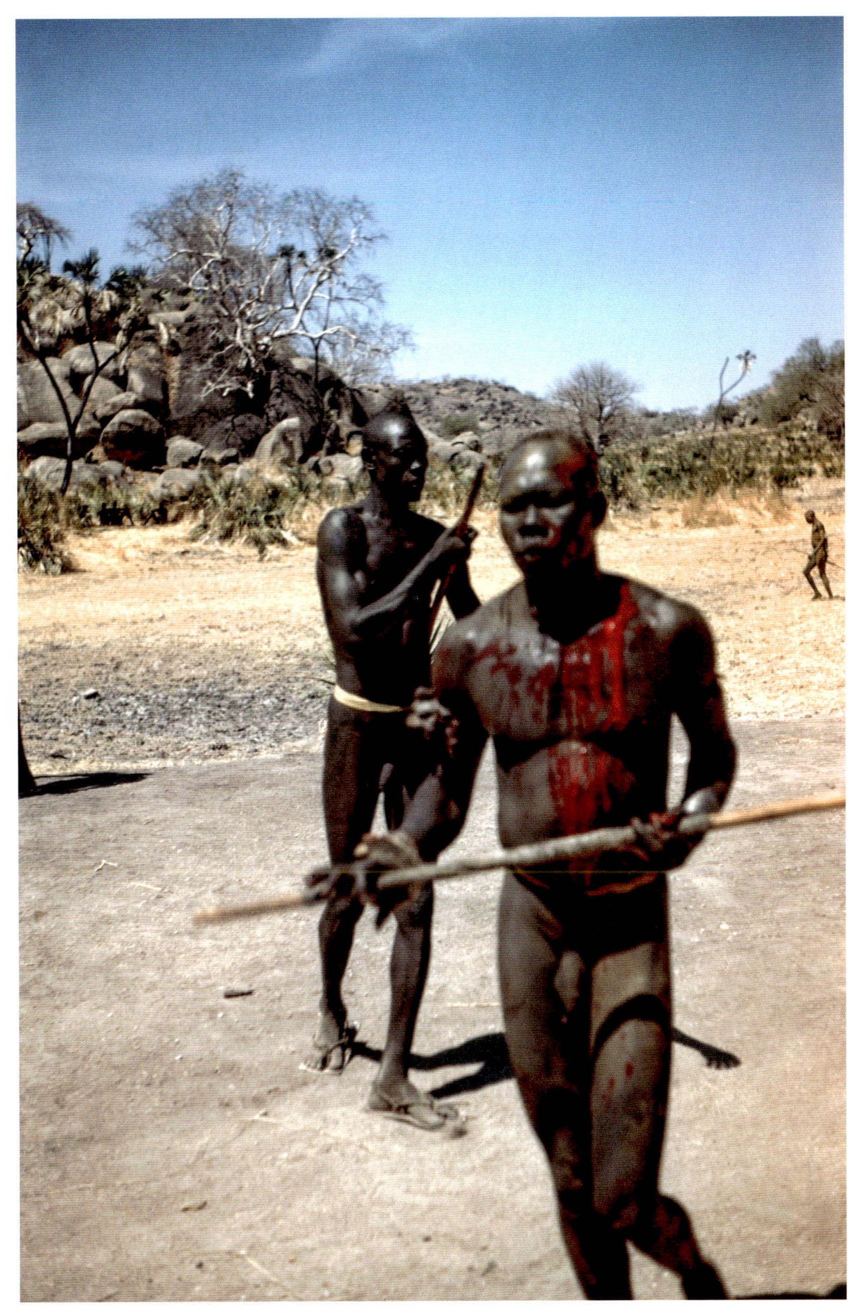

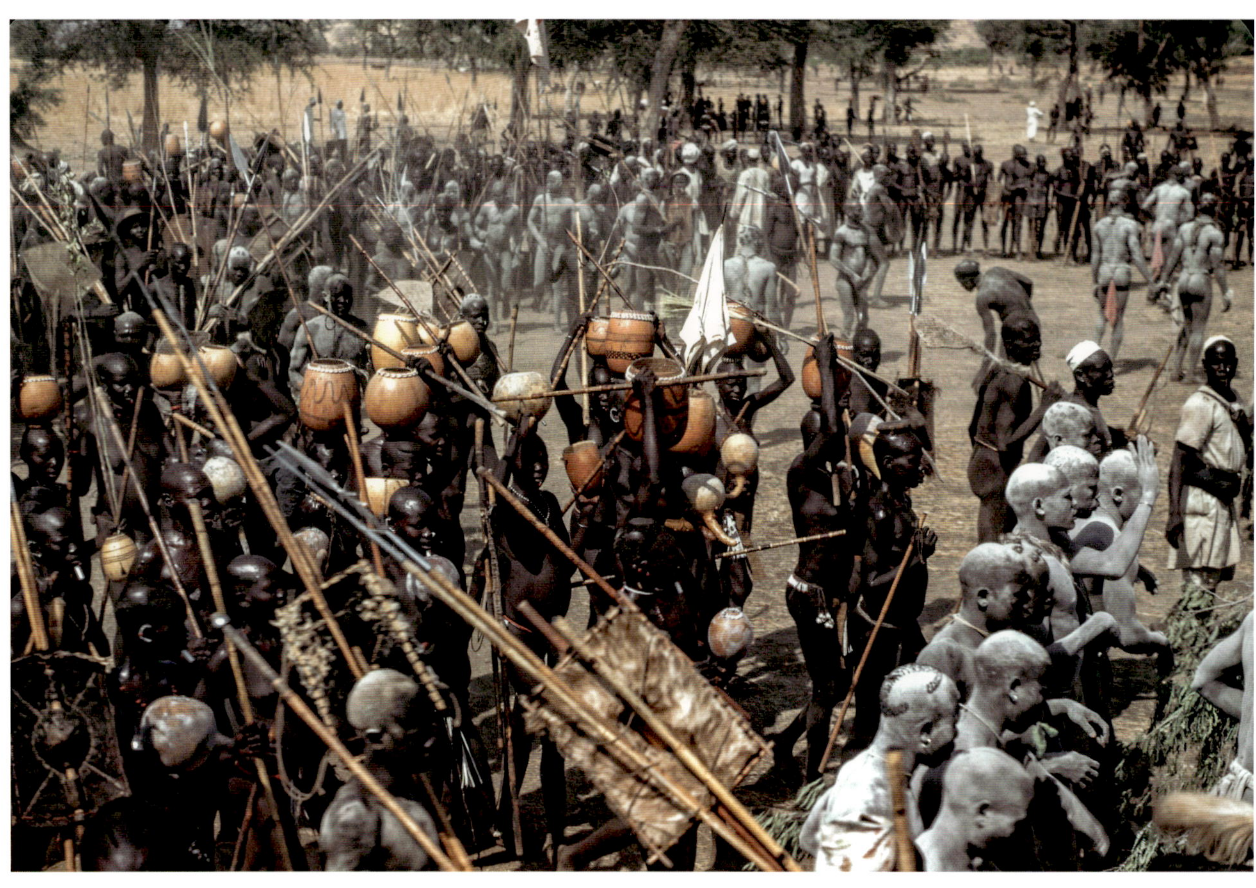

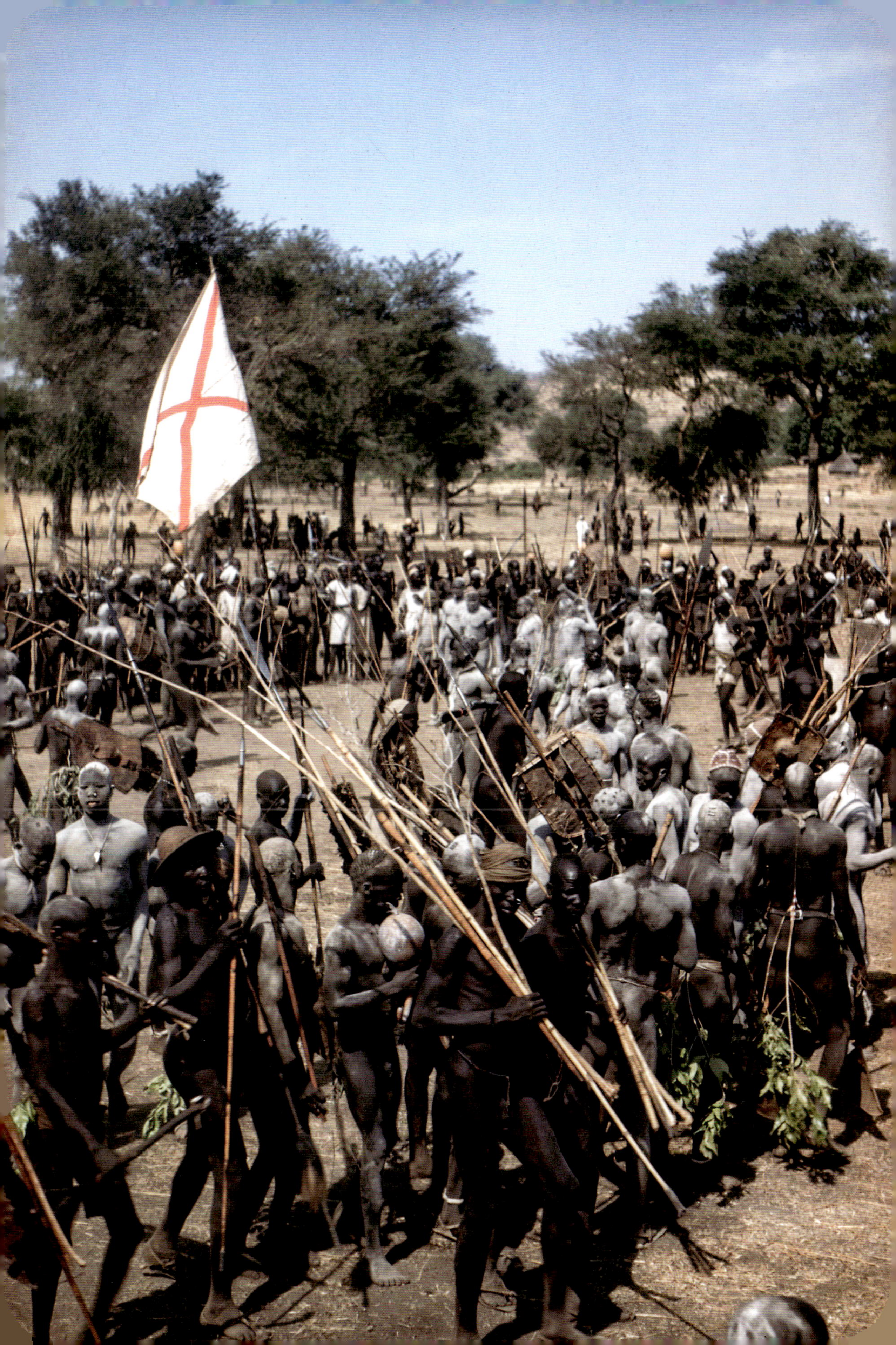

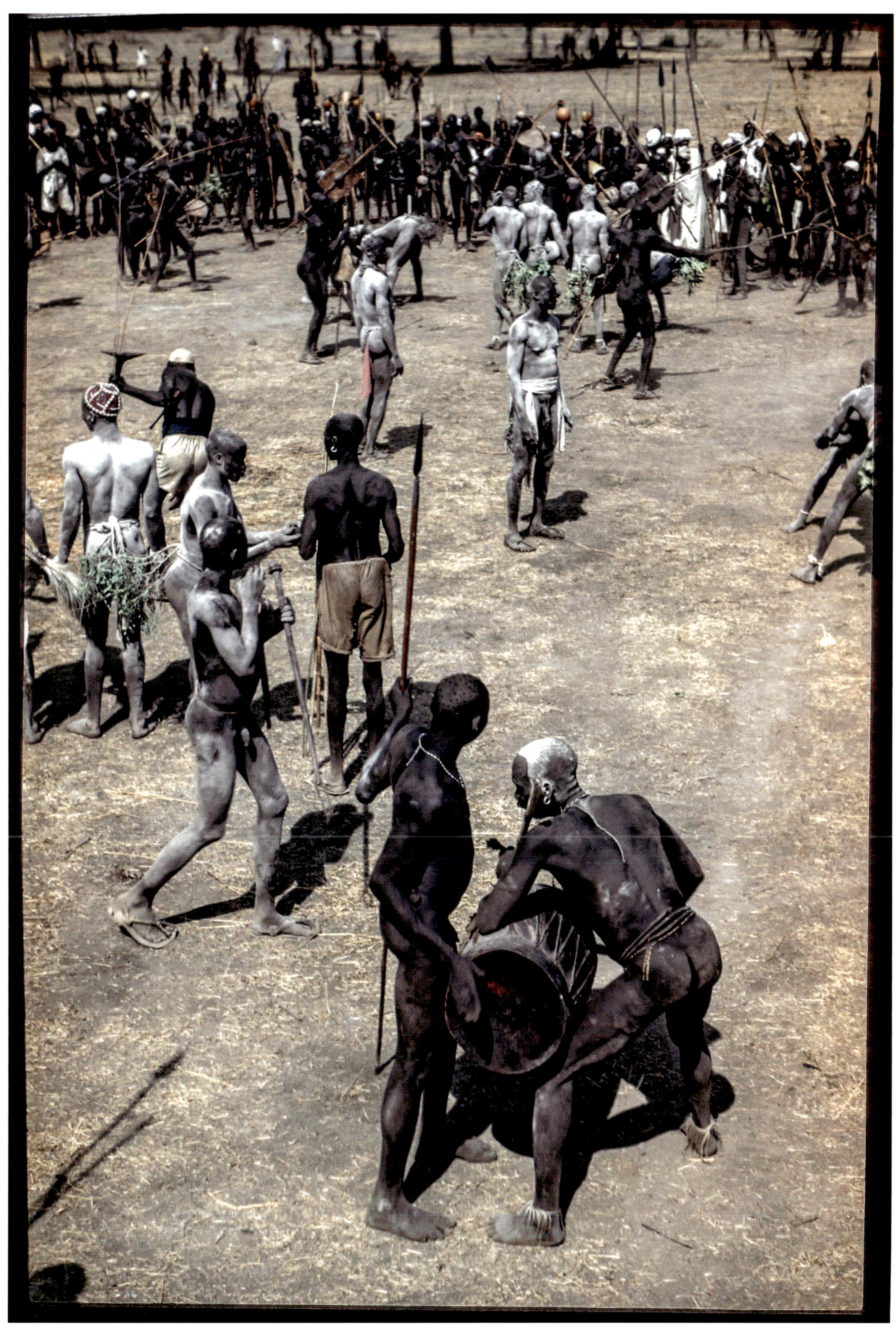

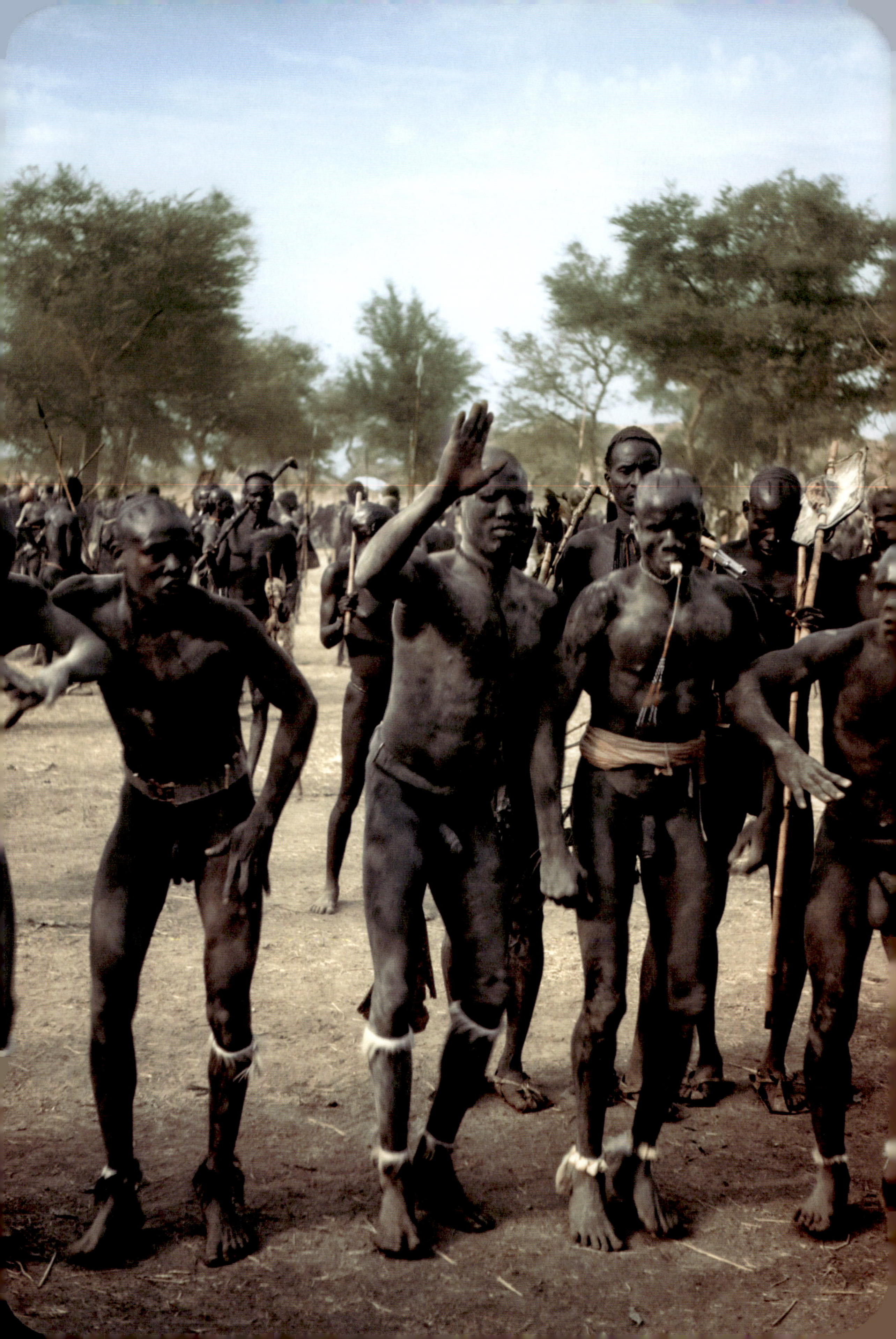

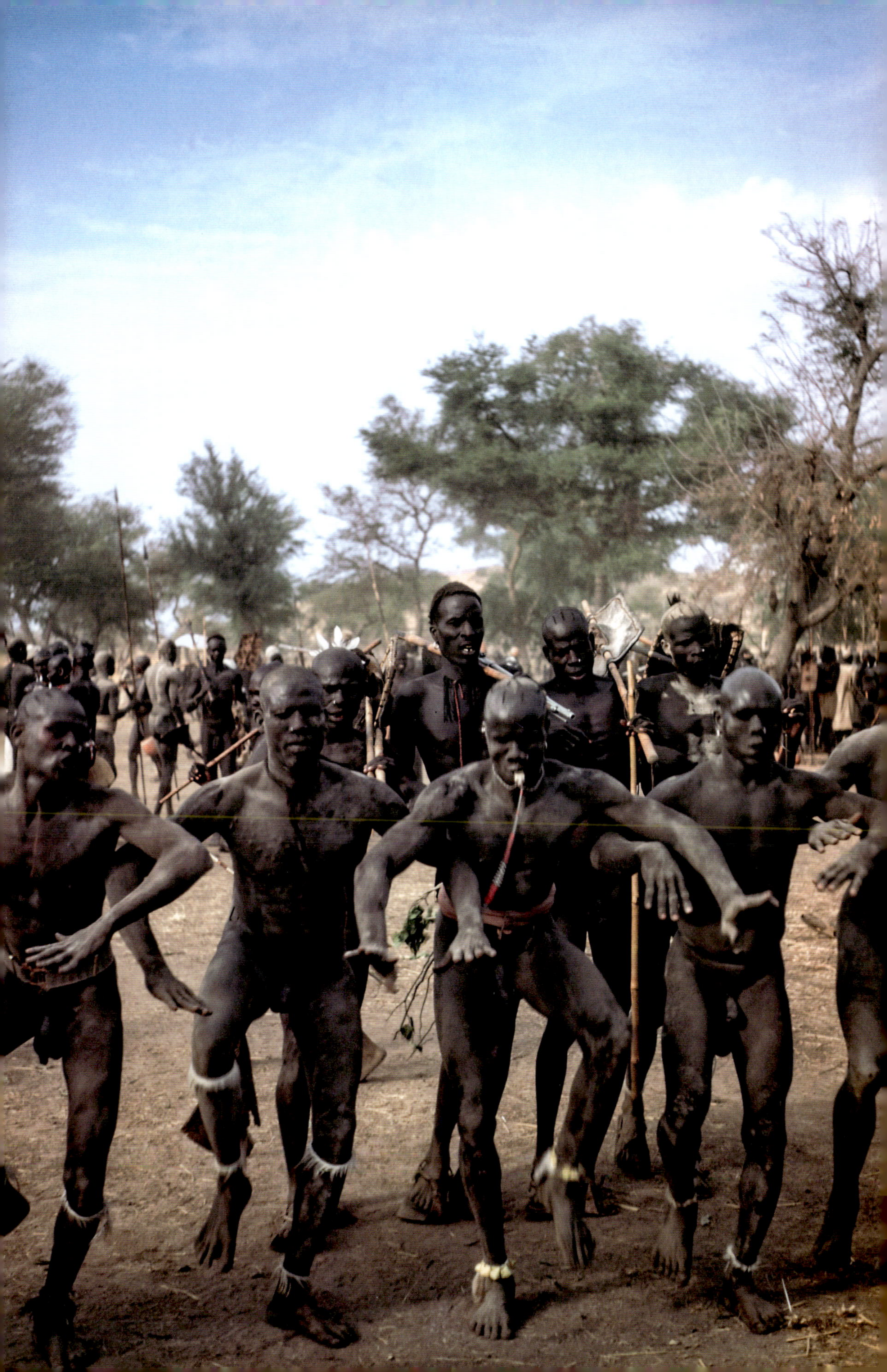

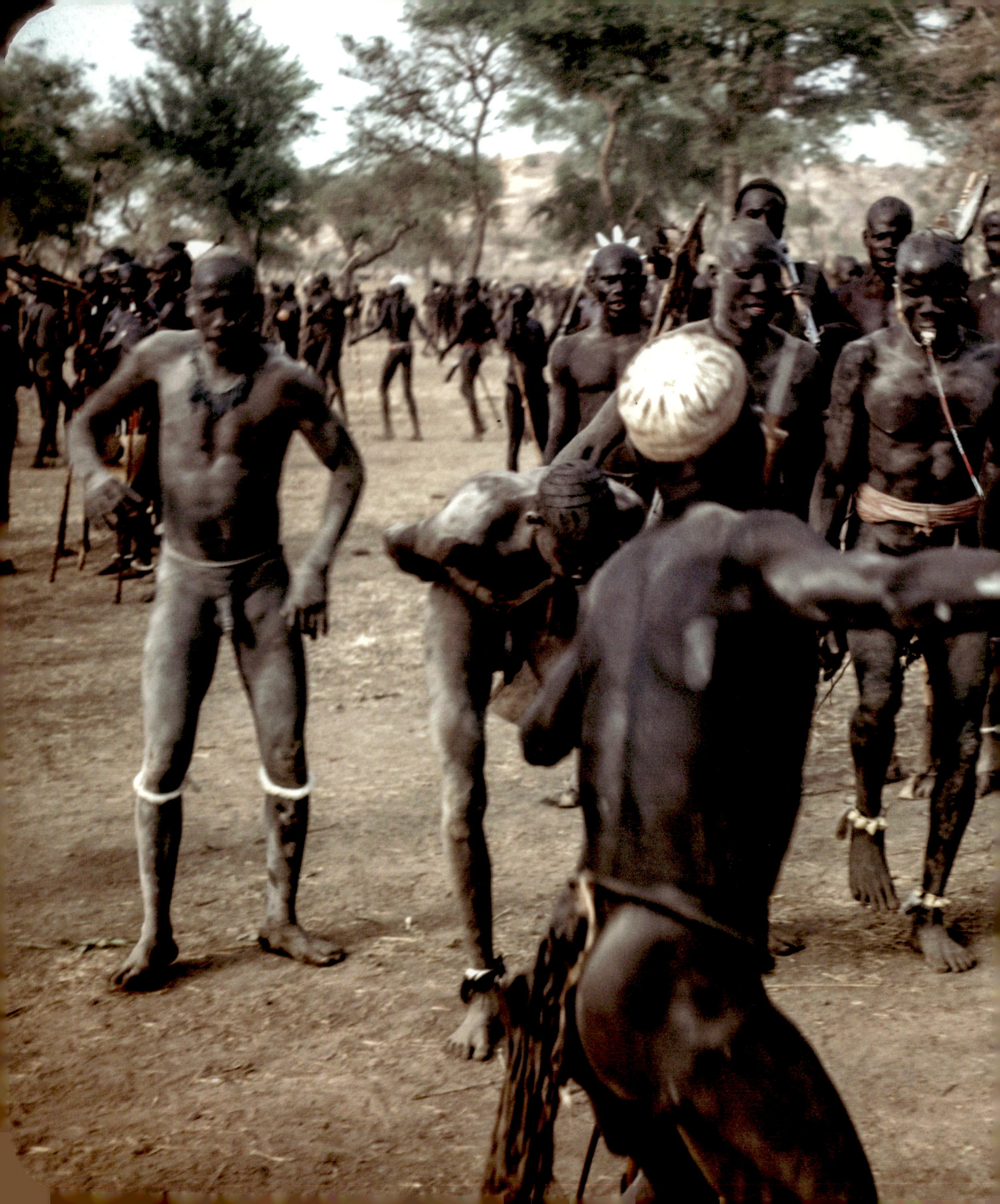

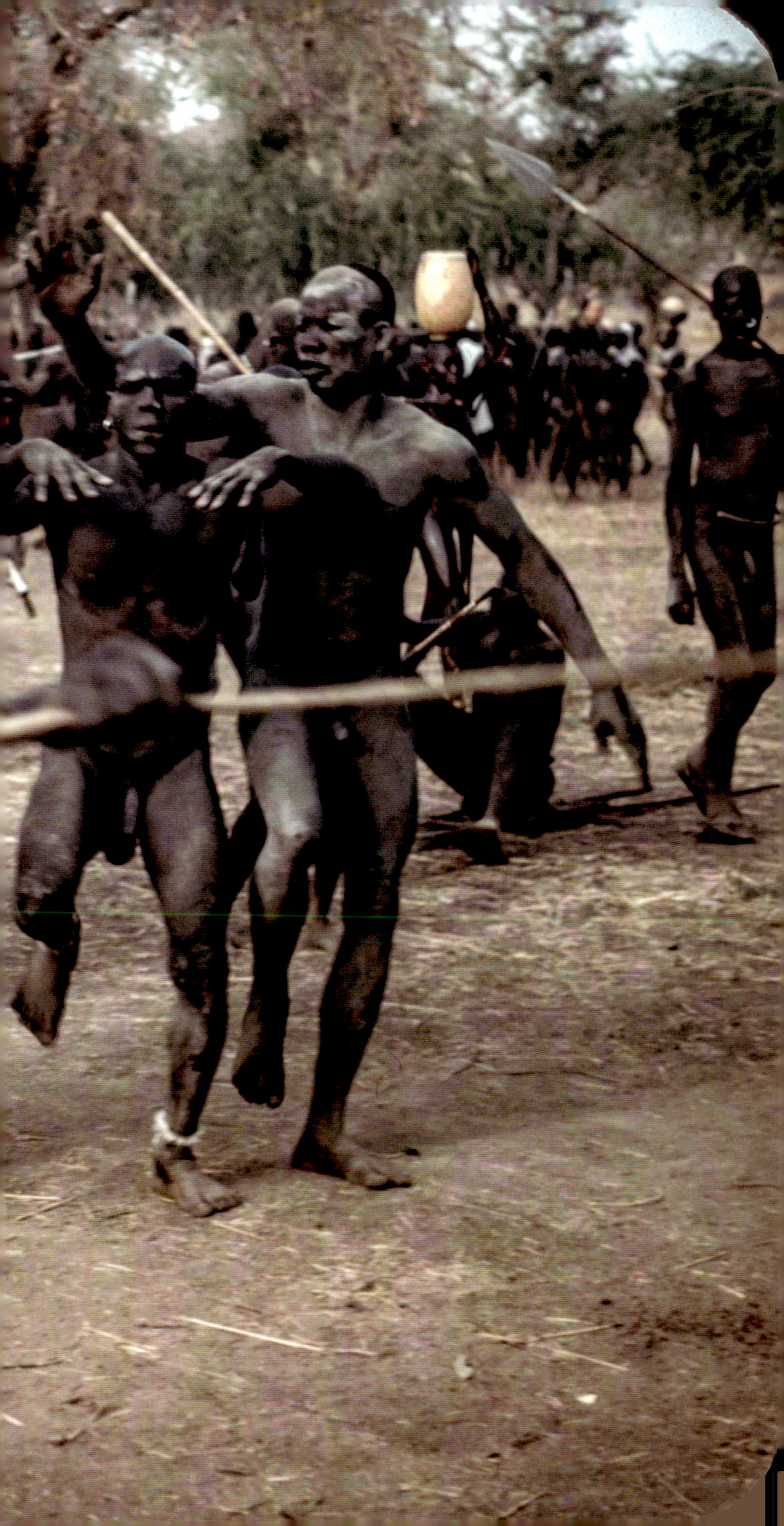

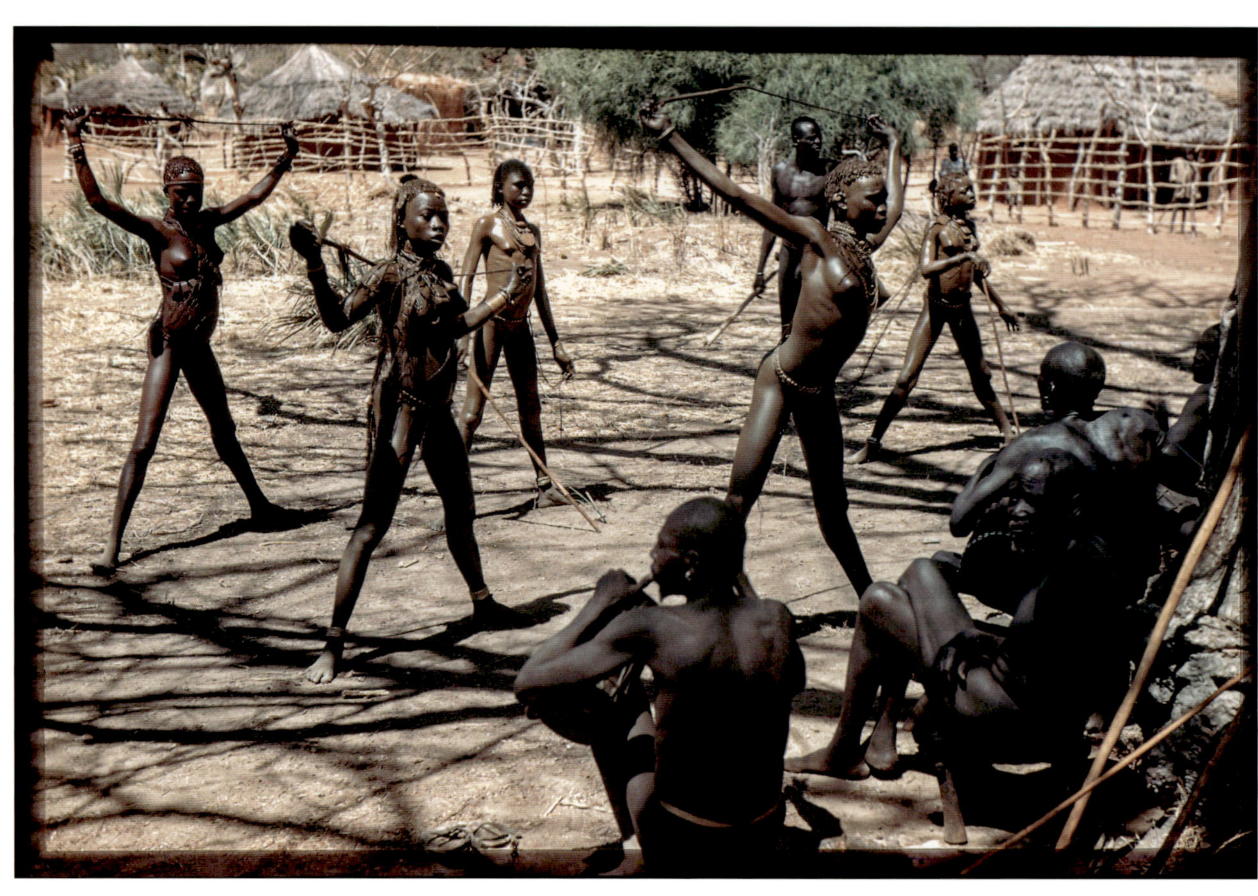

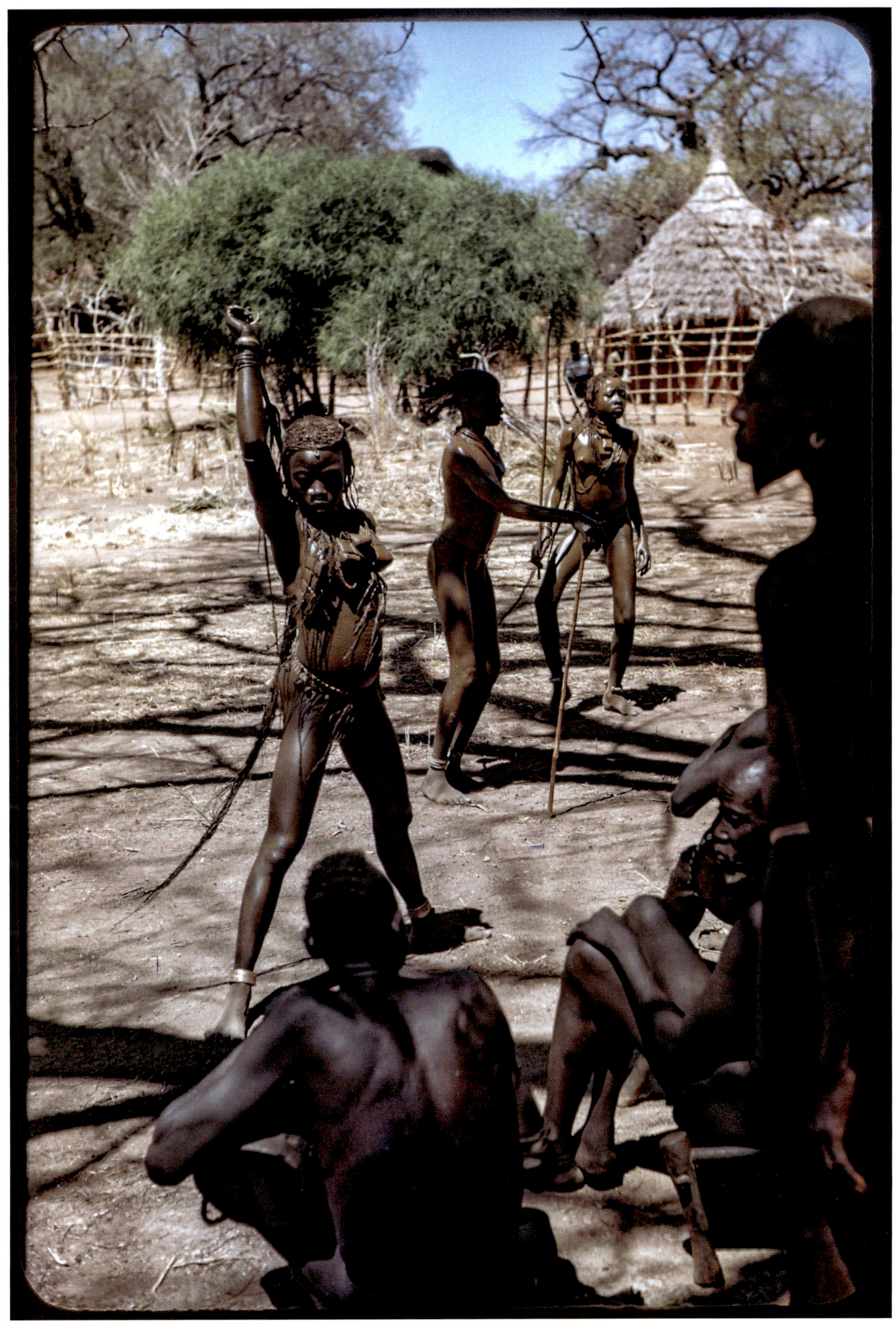

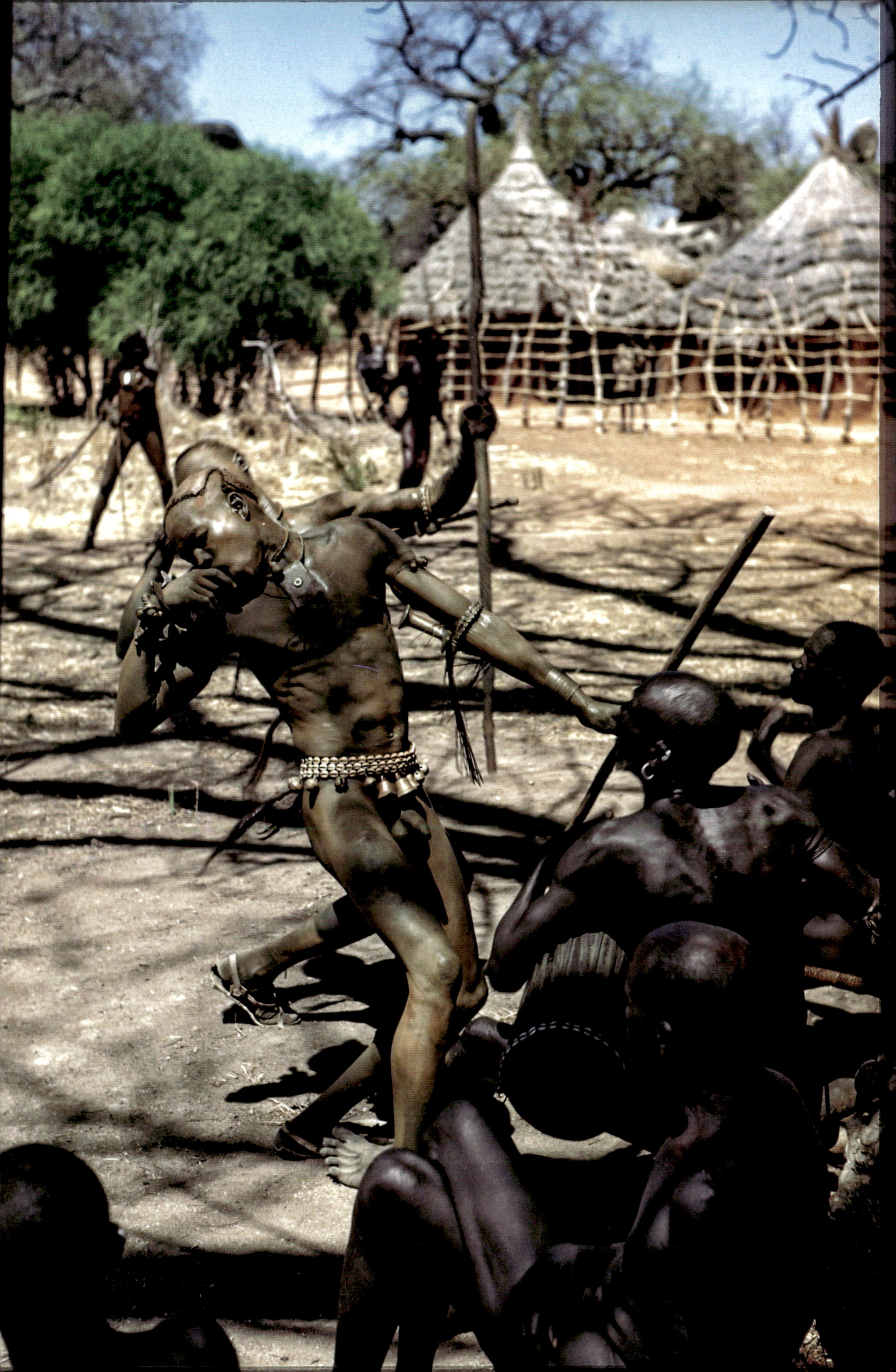

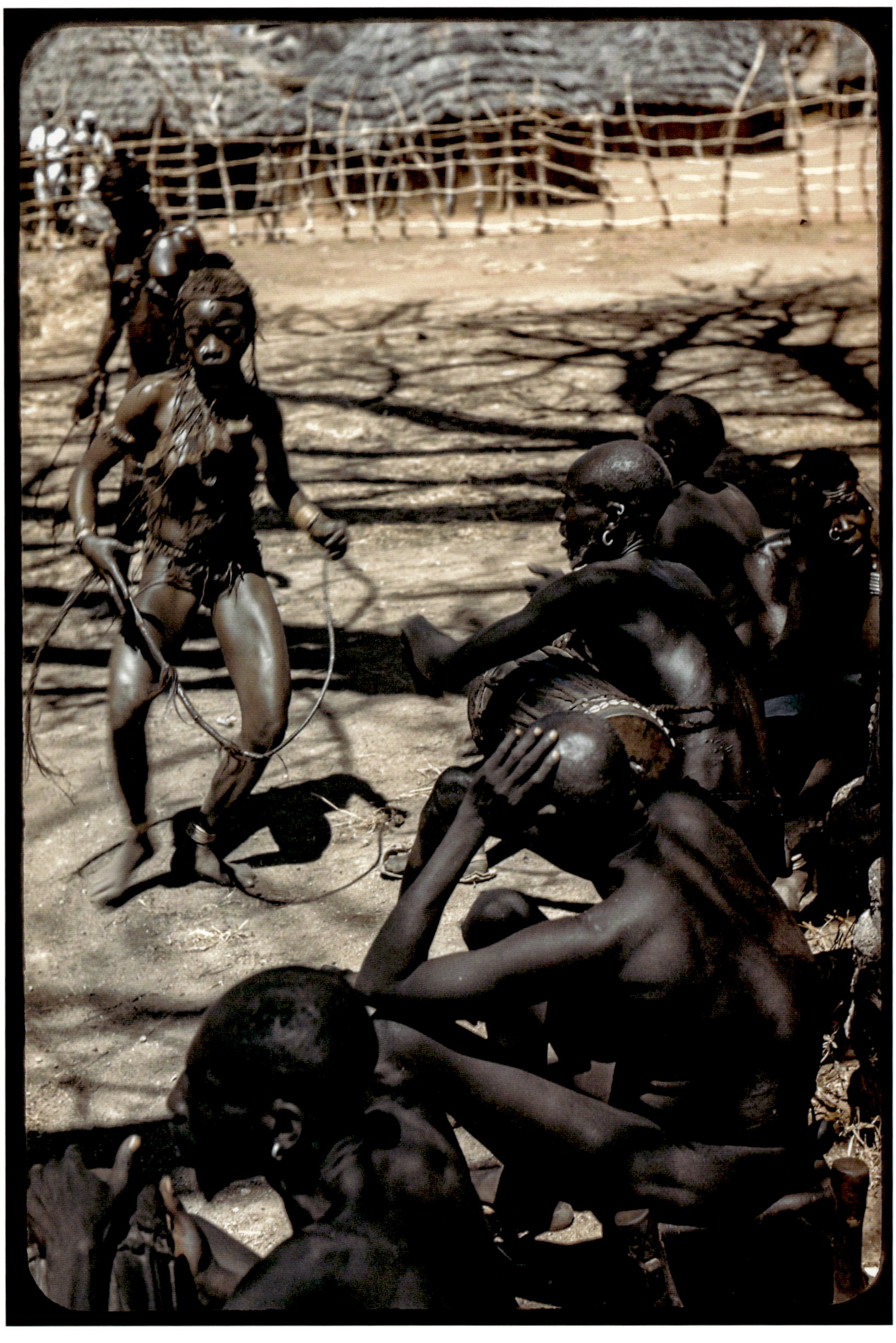

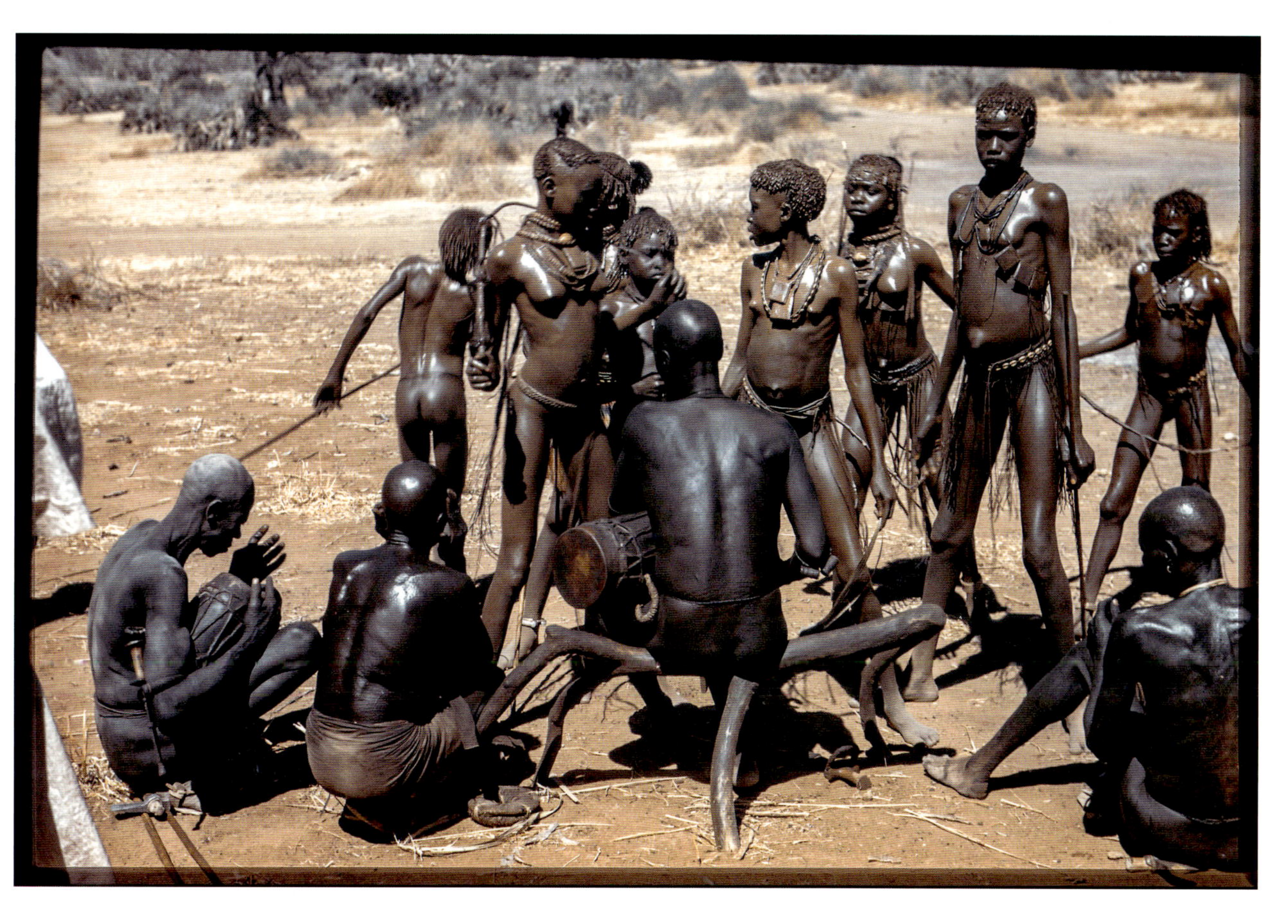

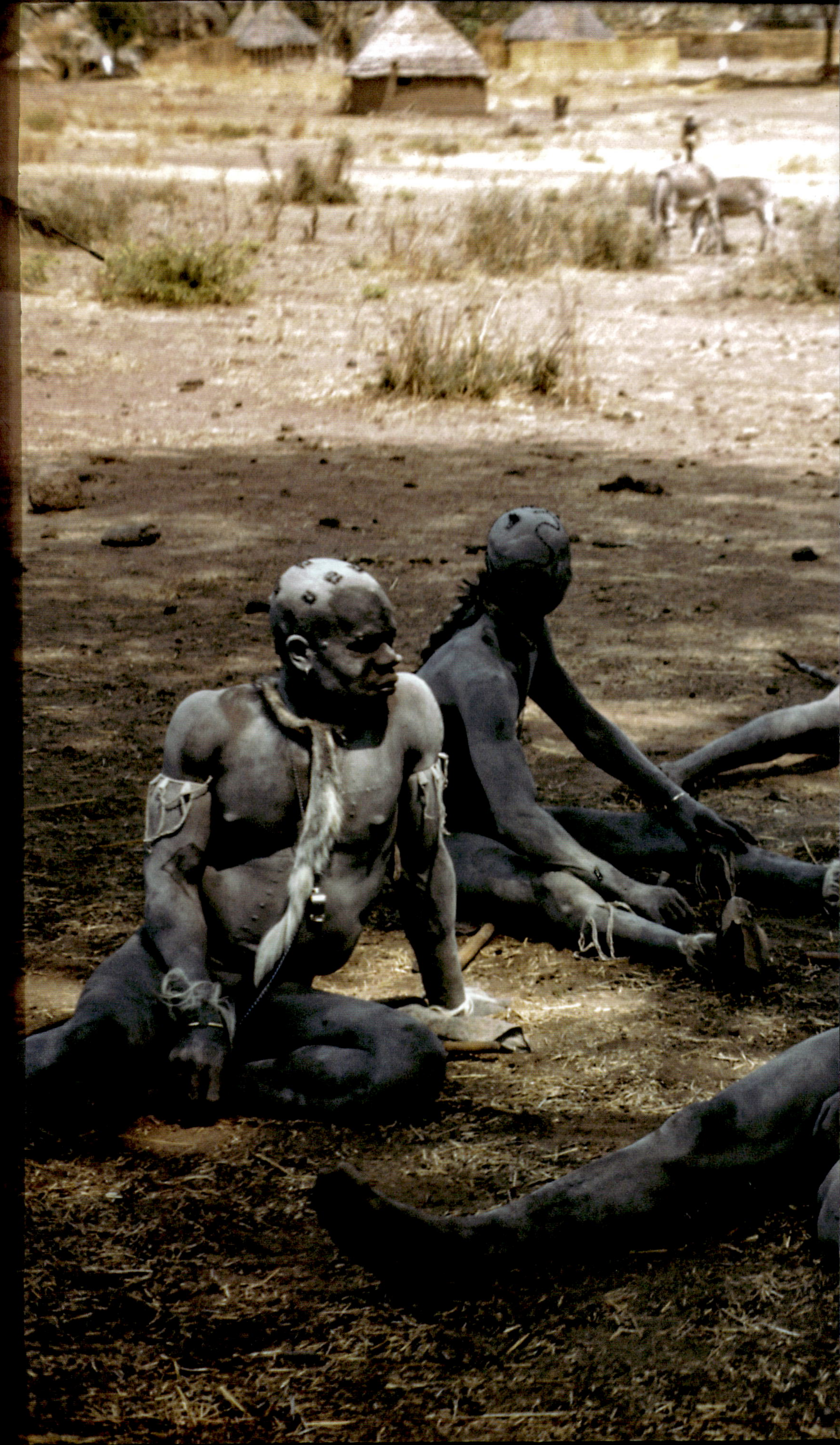

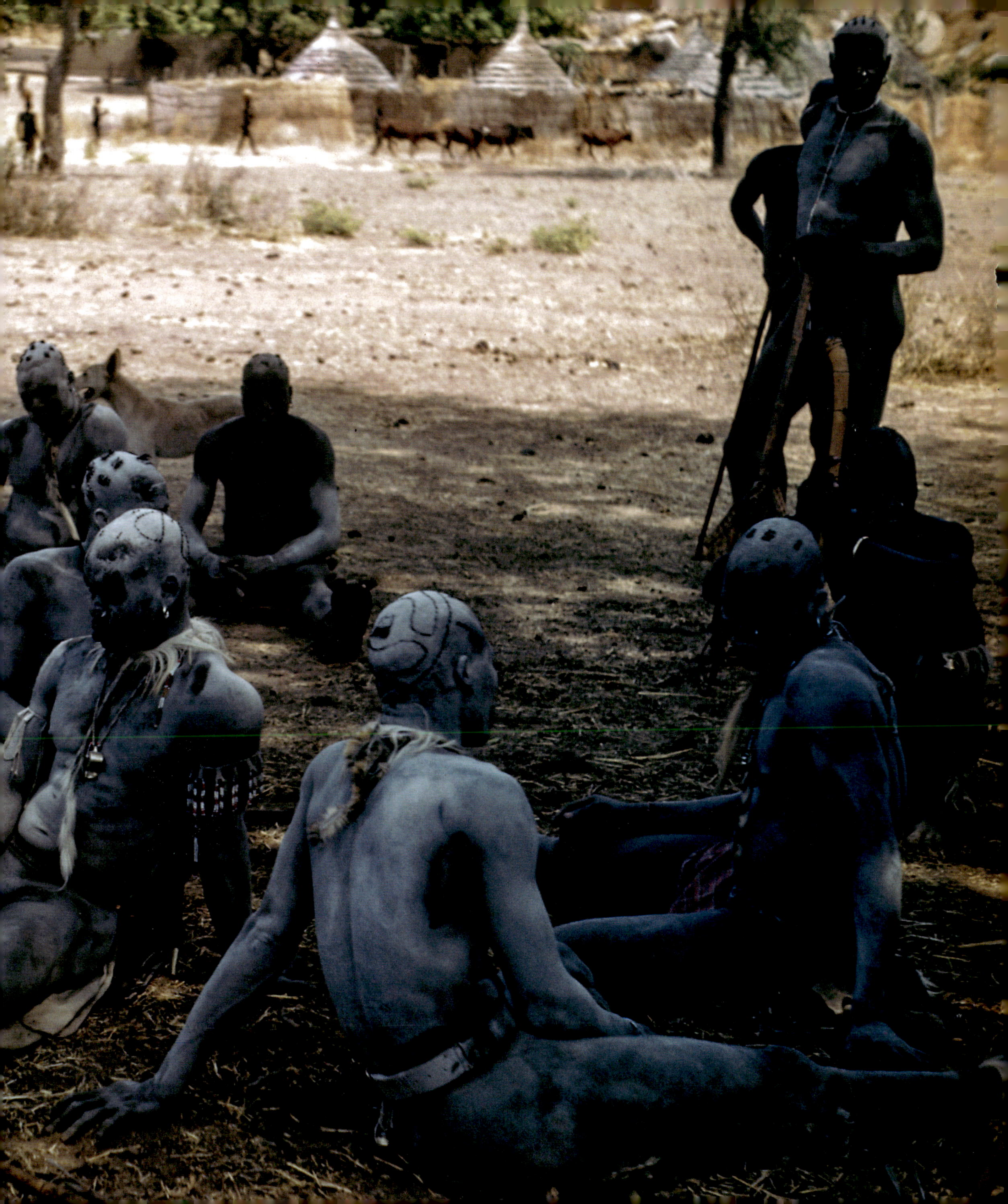

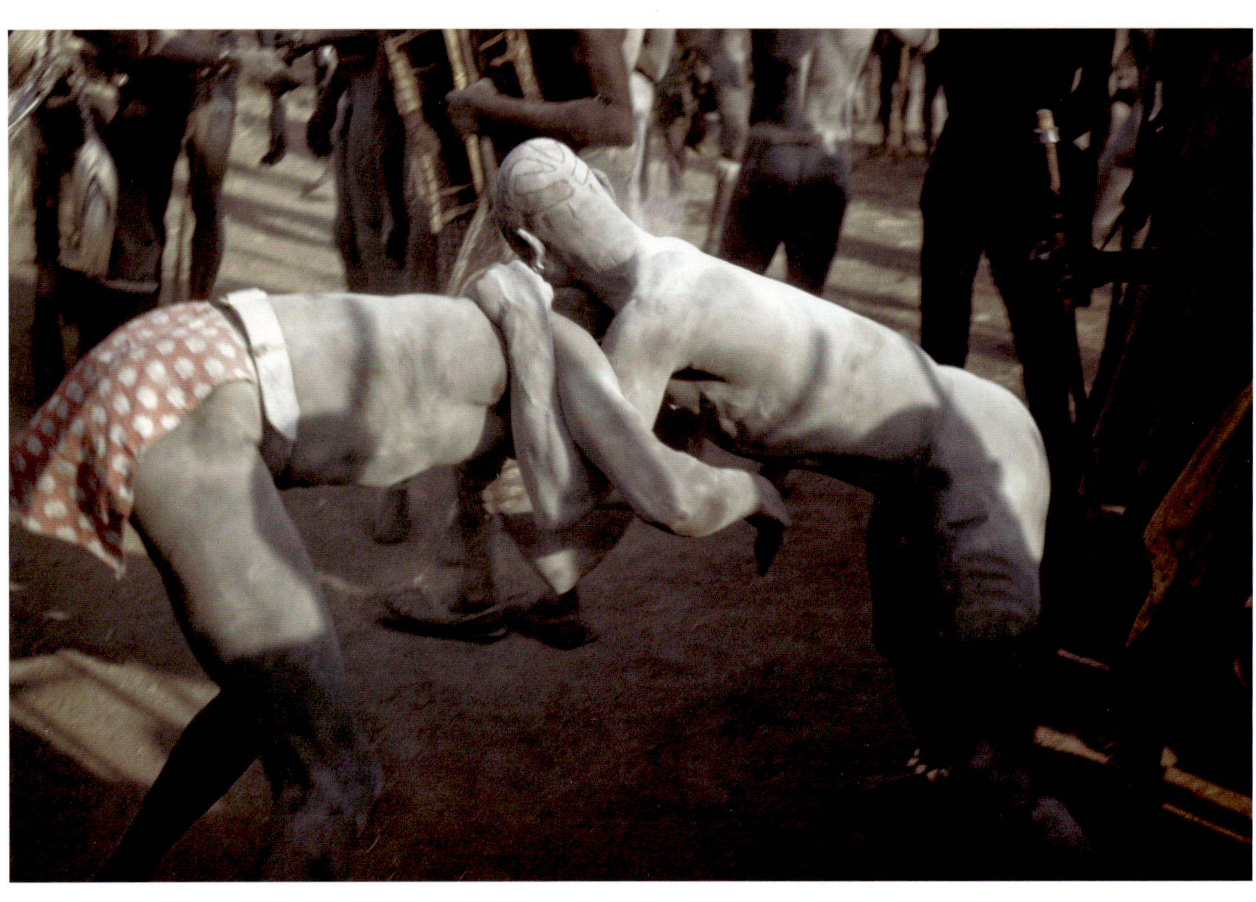

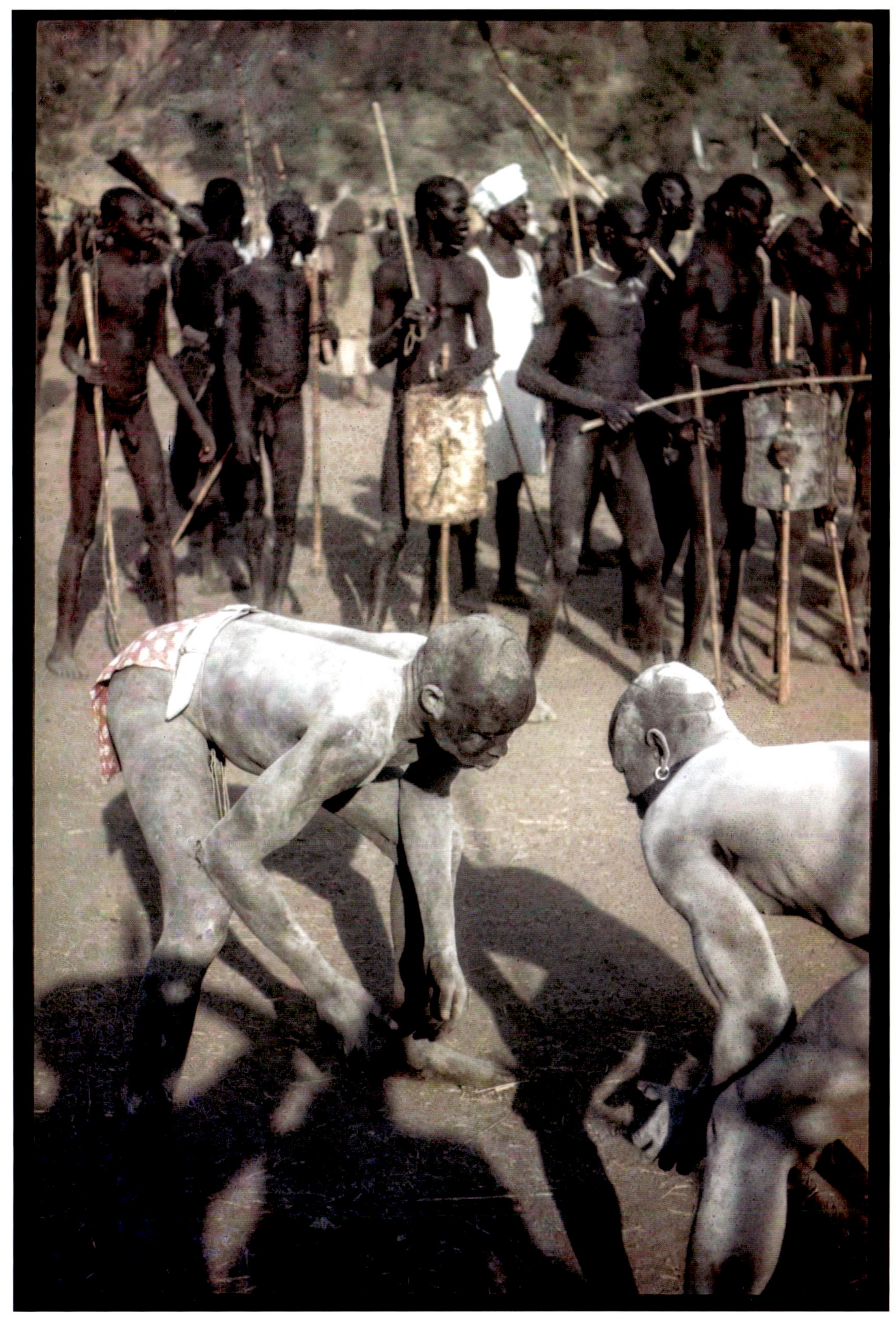

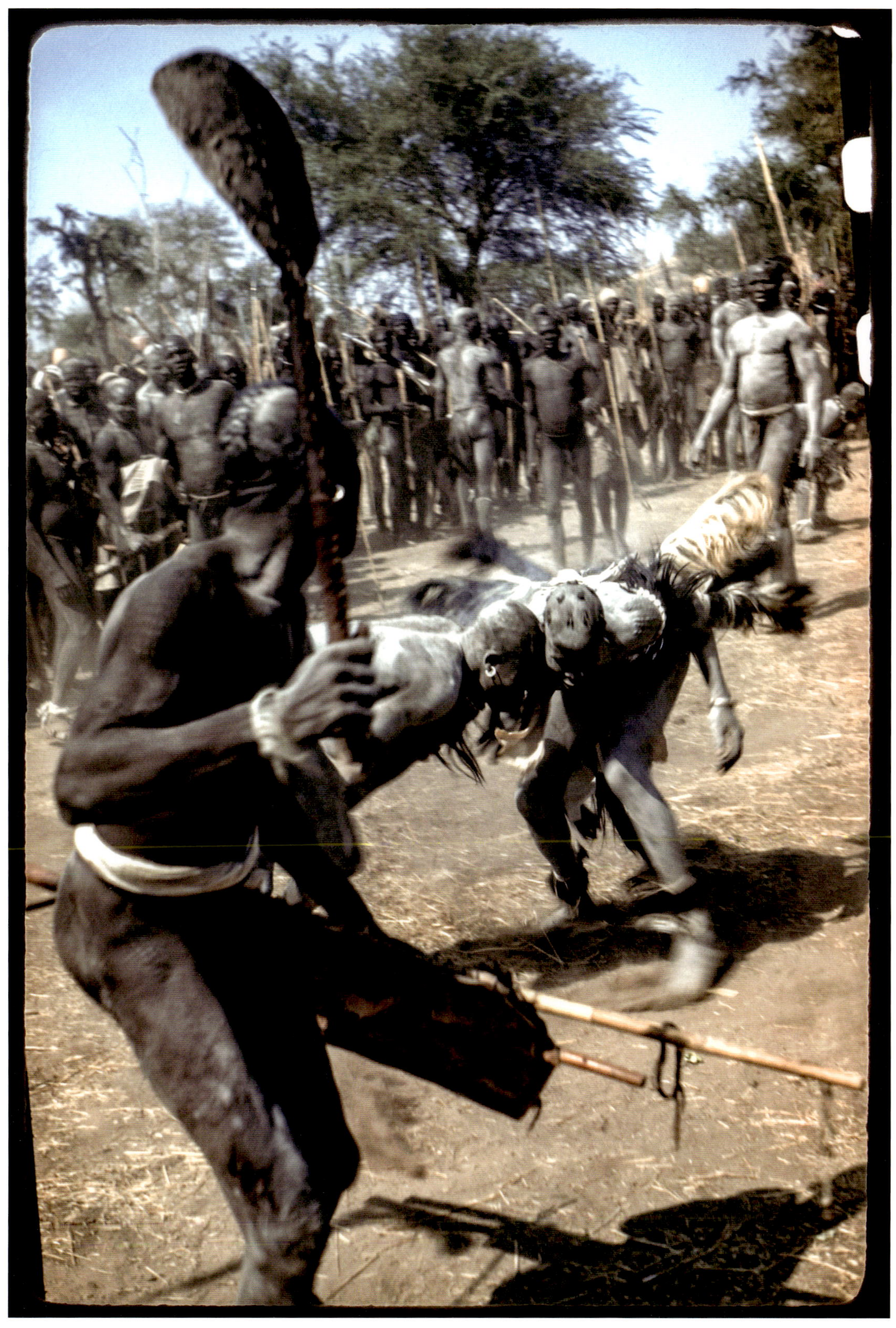

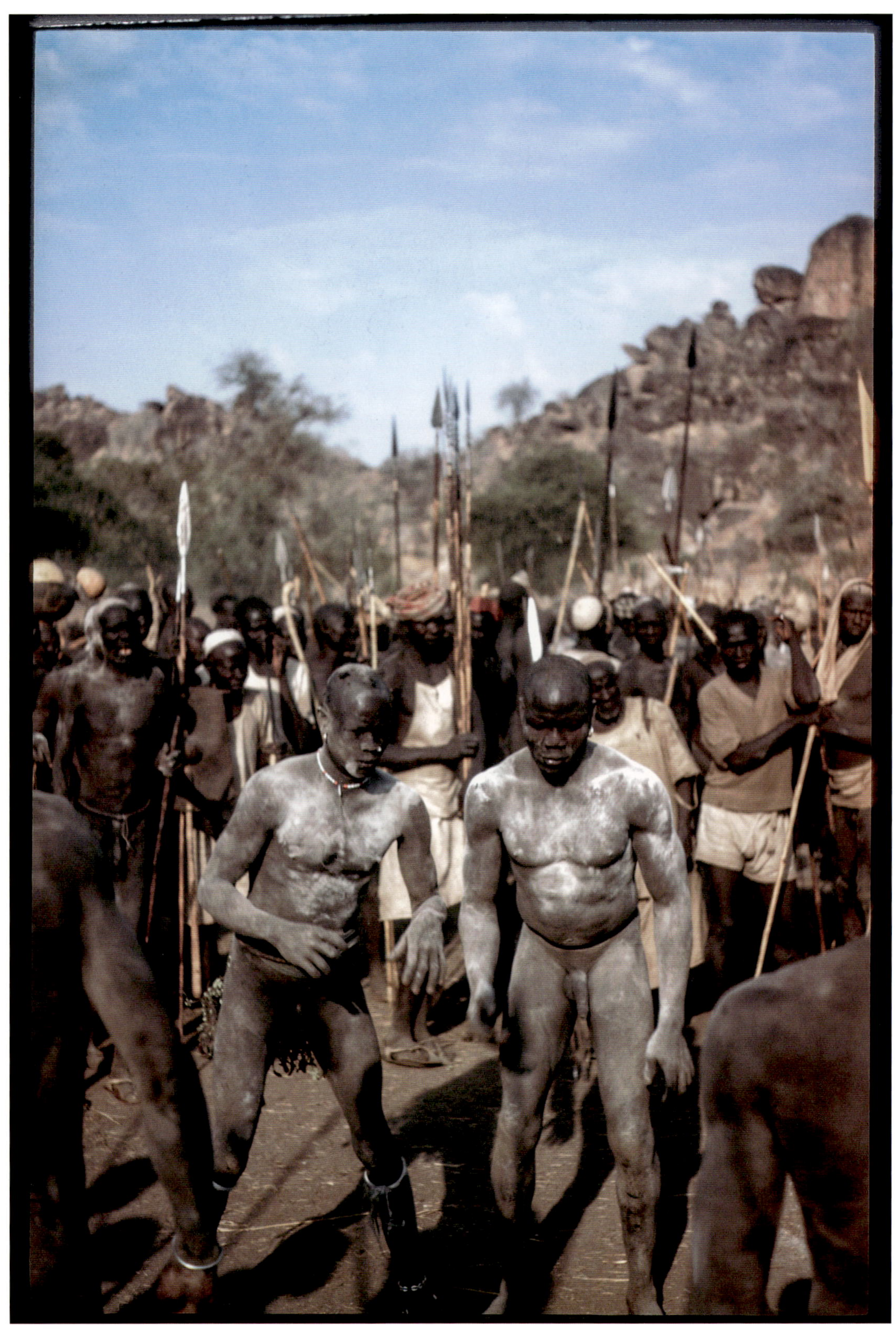

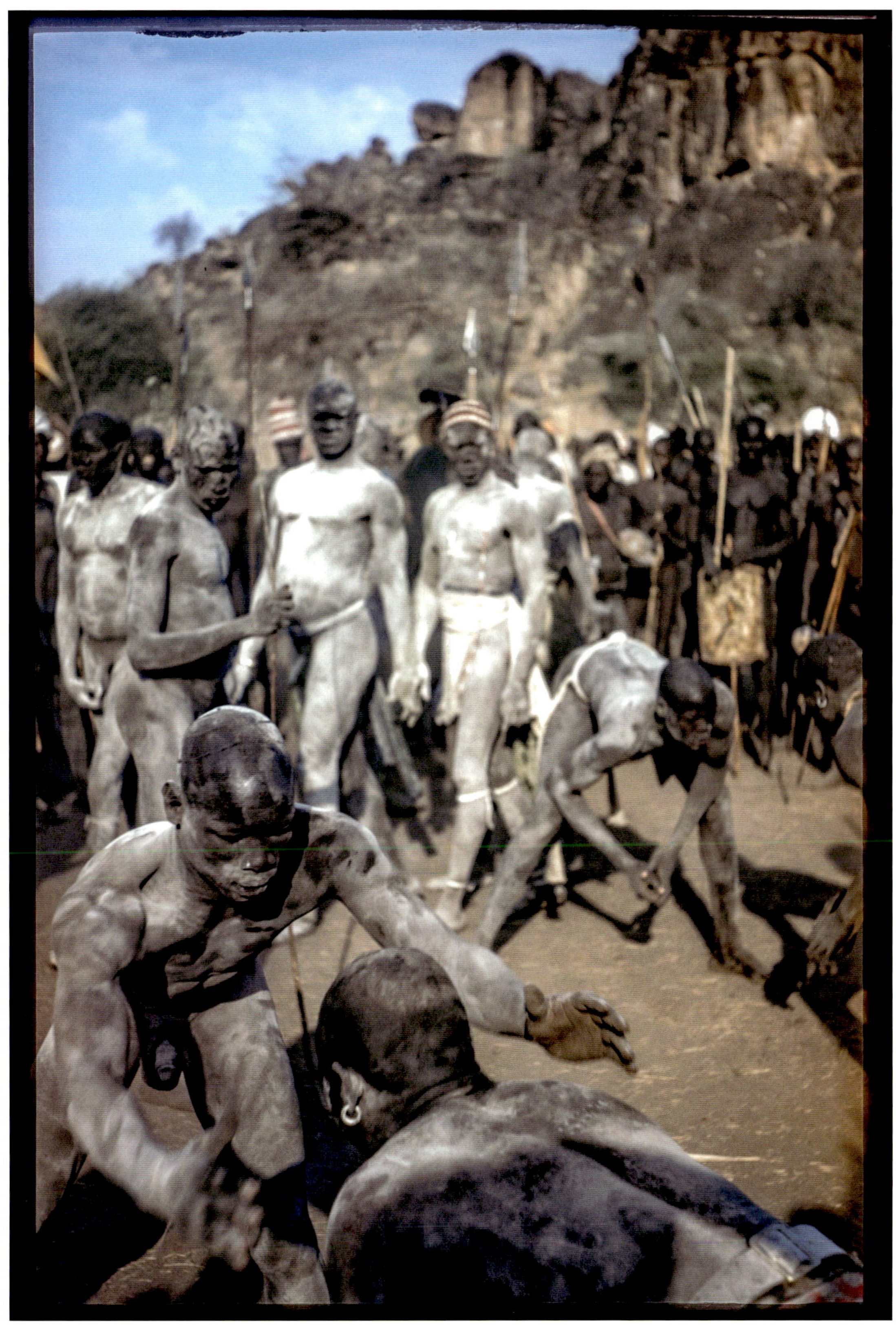

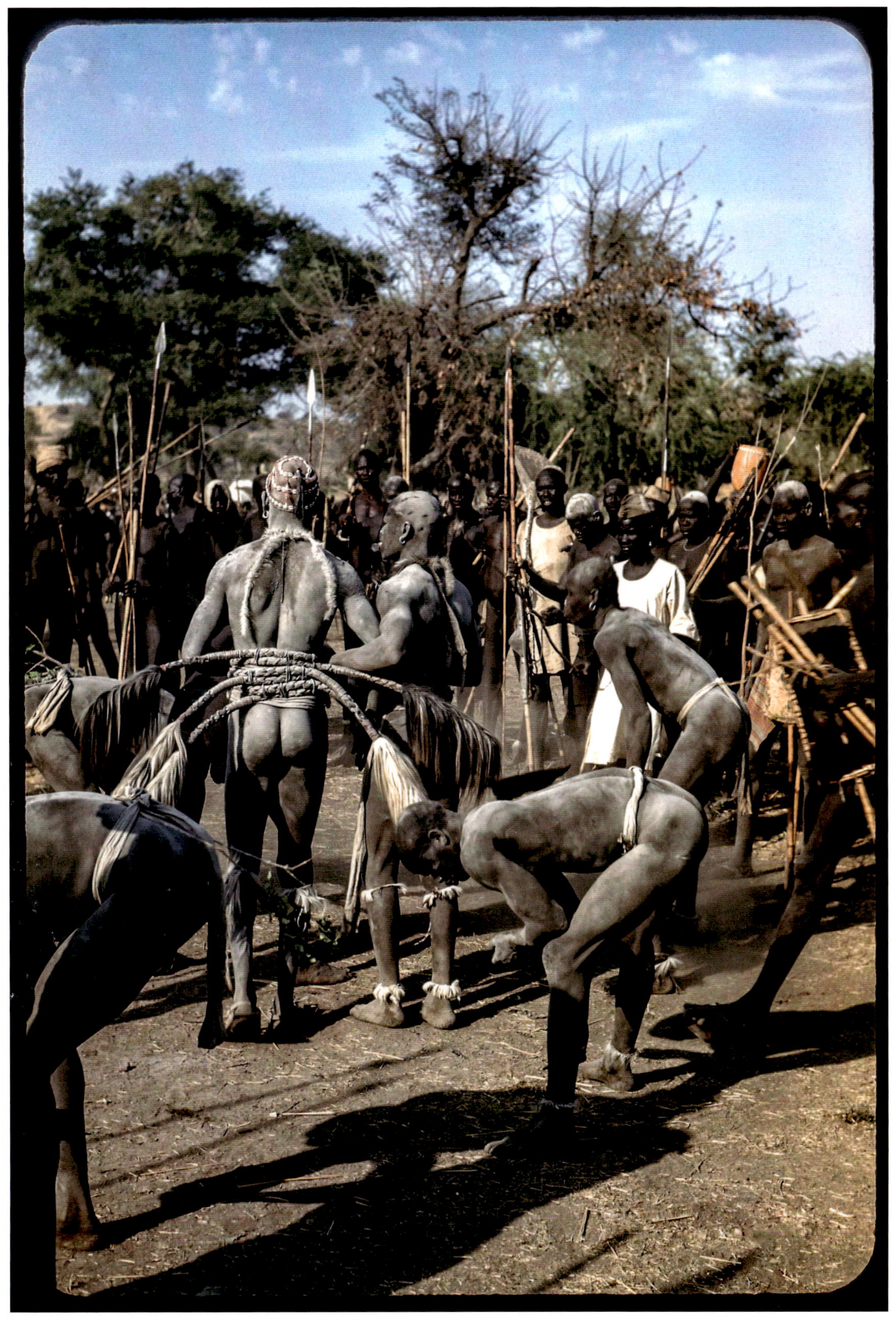

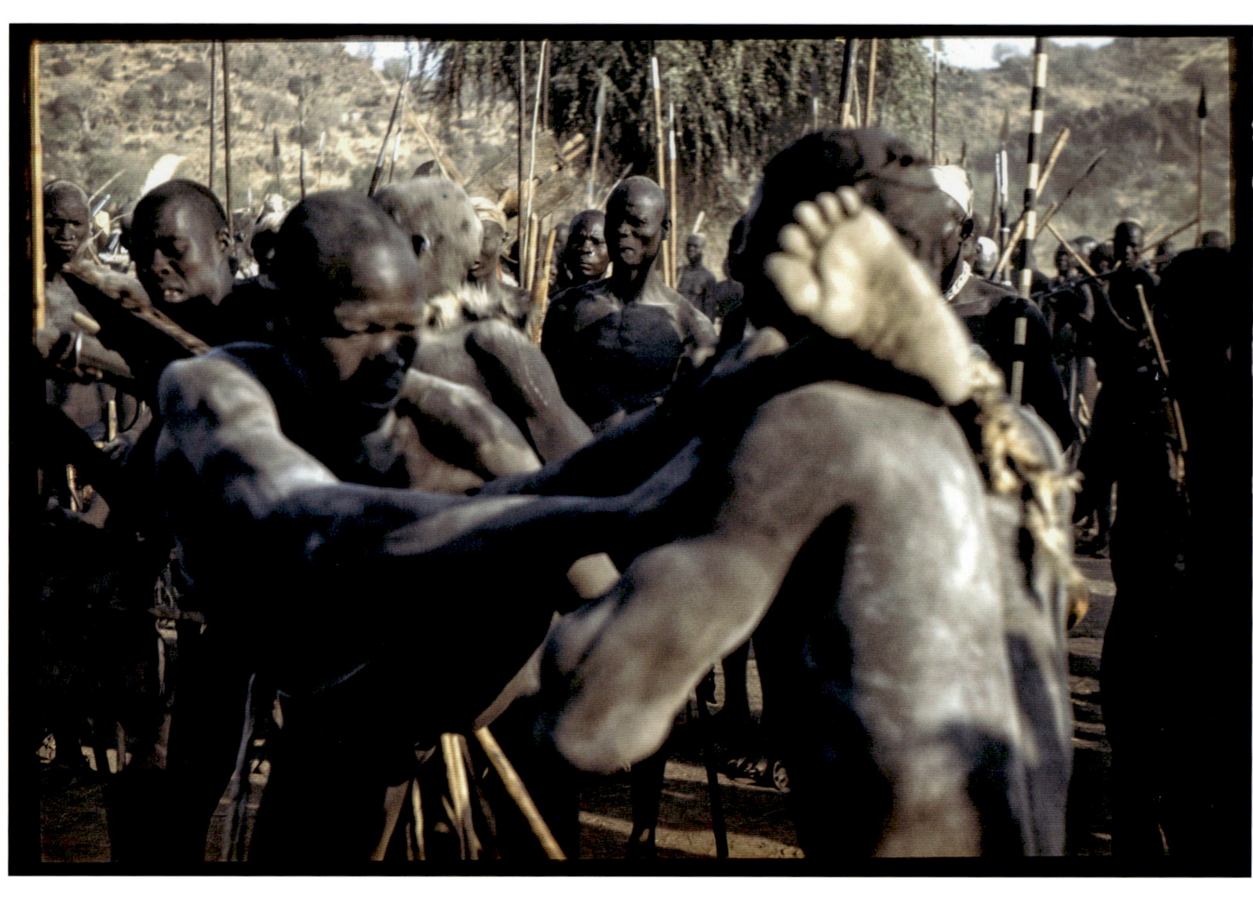

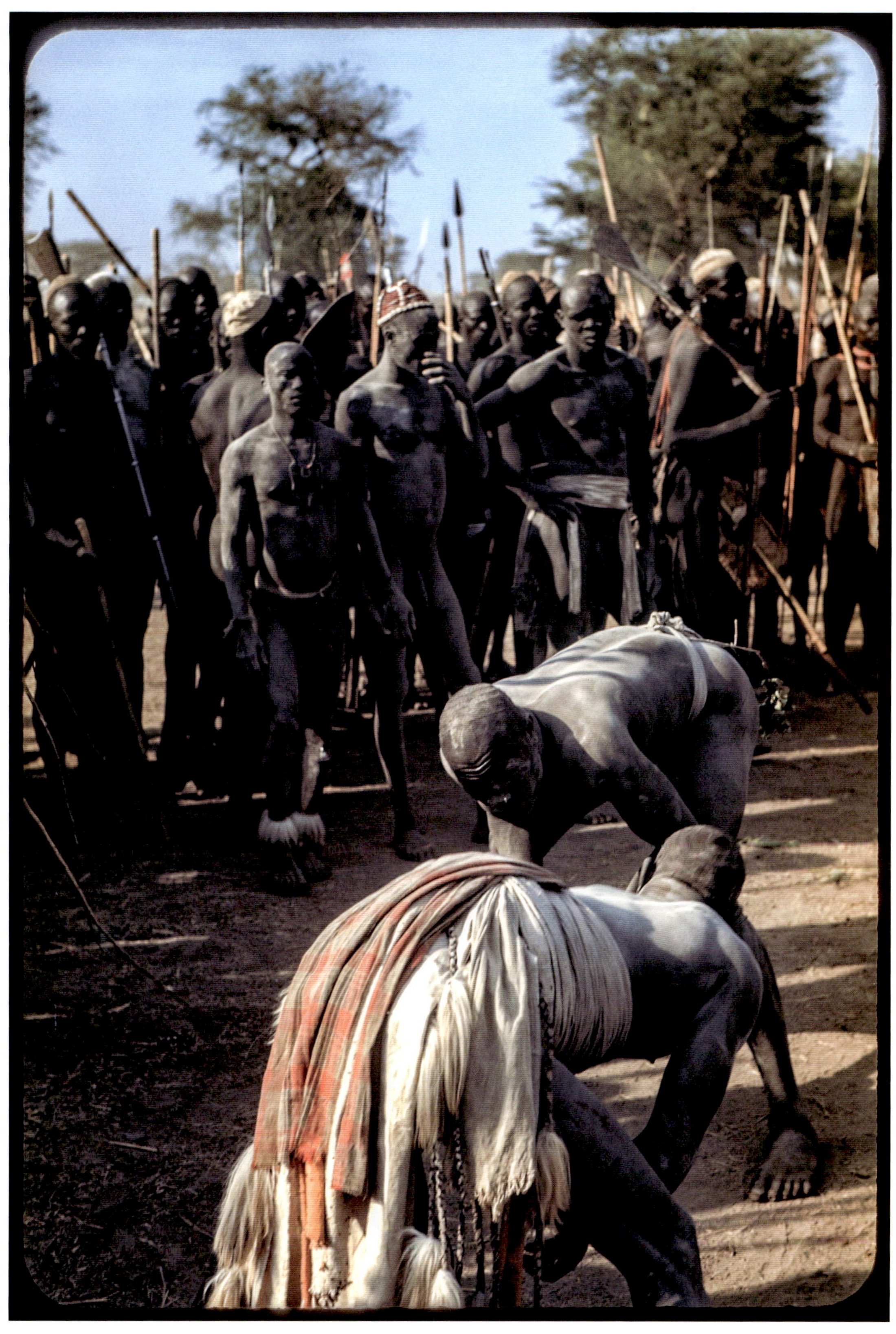

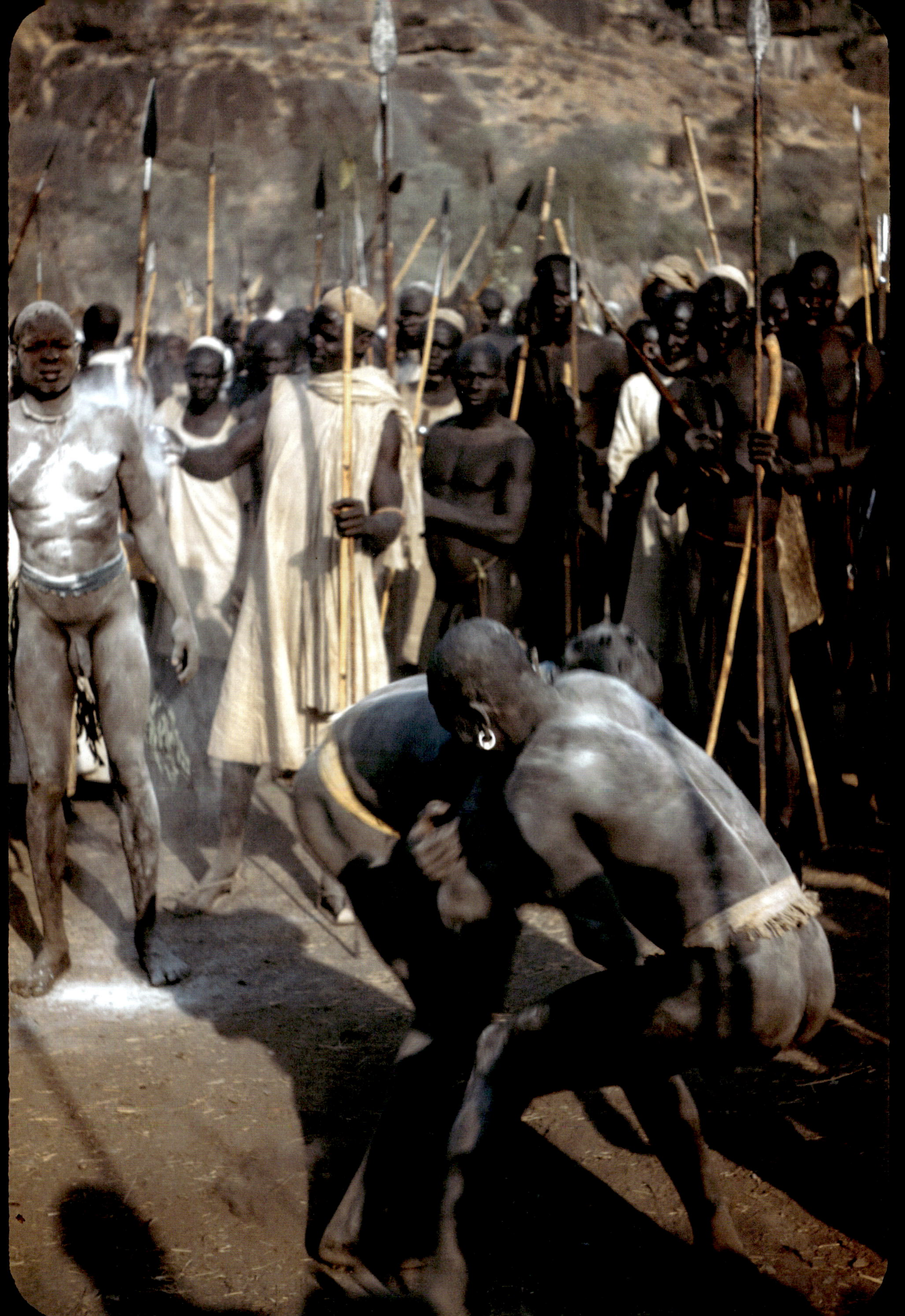

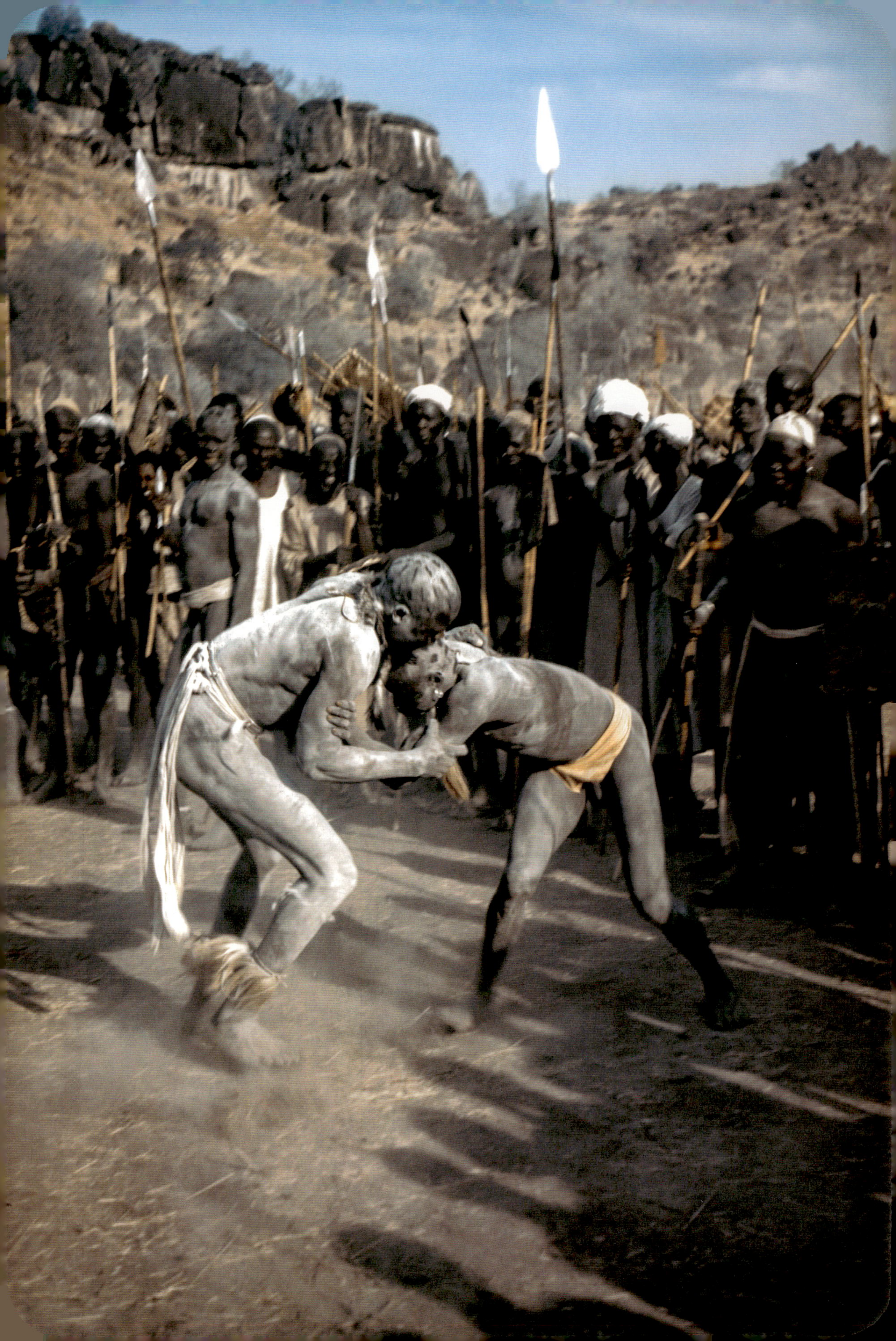

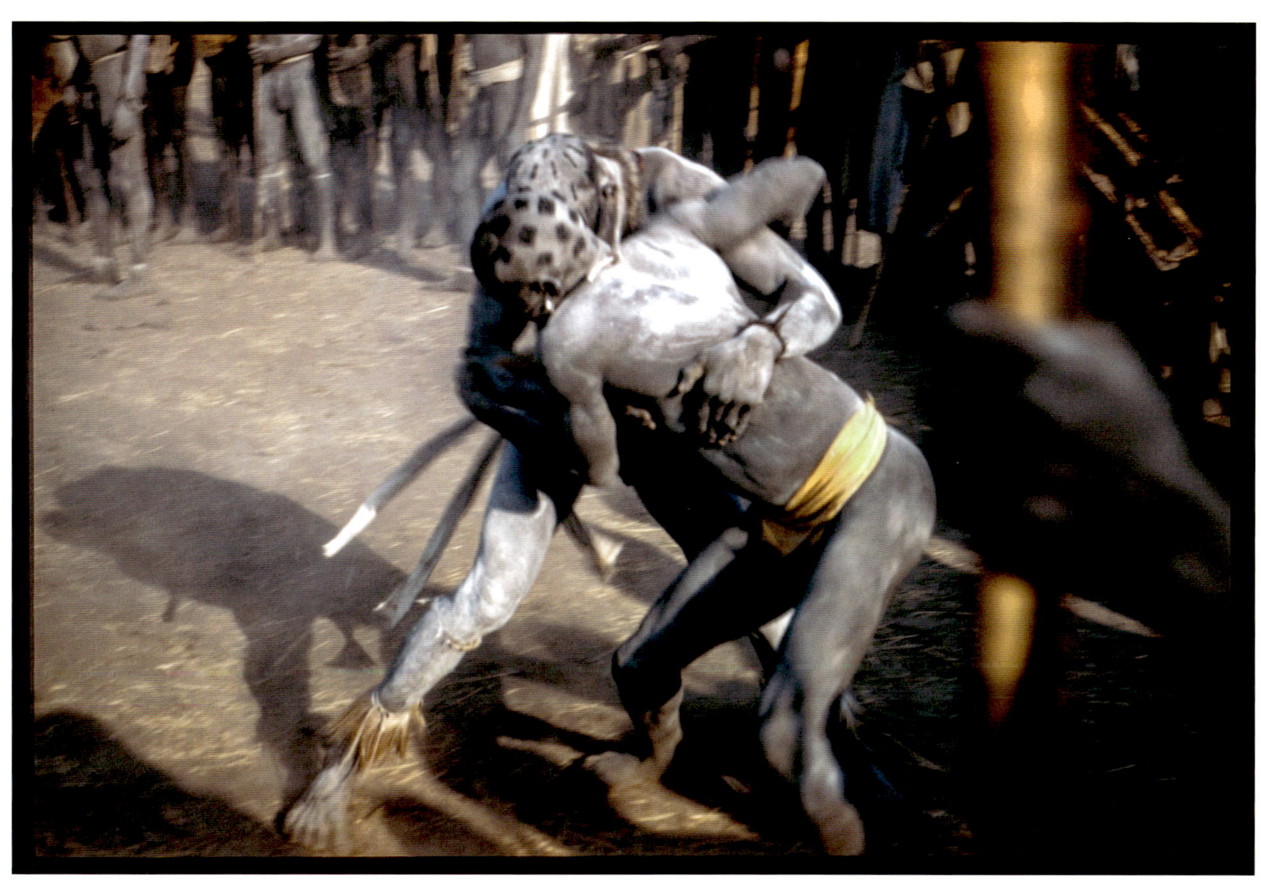

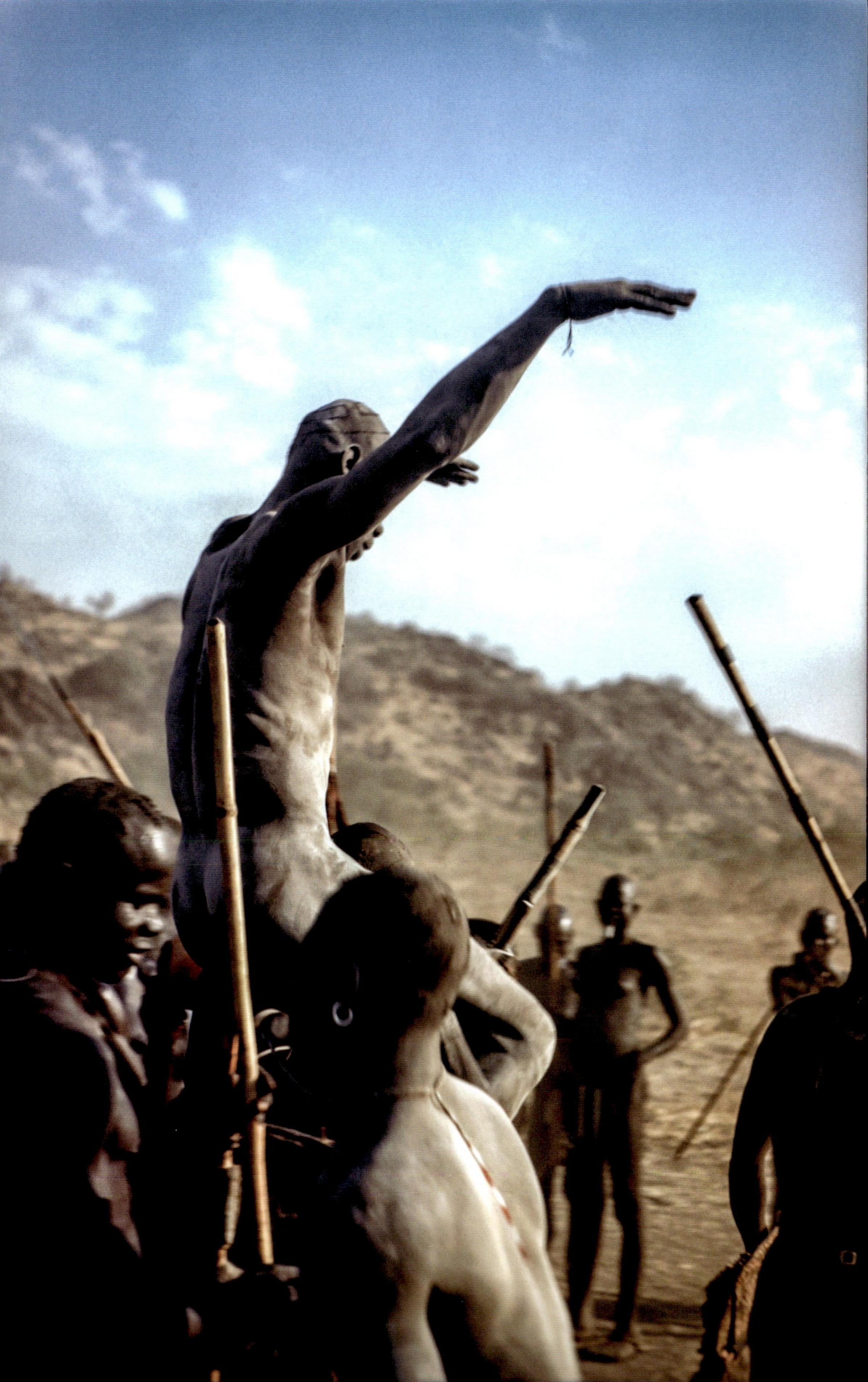

CAPTIONS

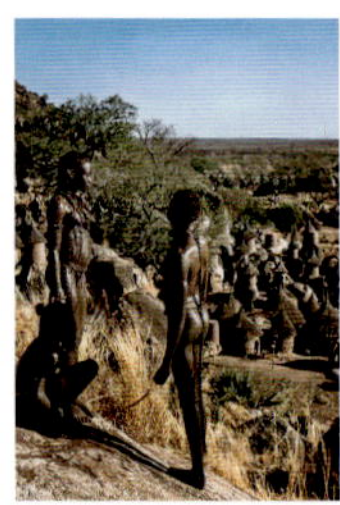

5

Girl dancers from the village of Kao. 1949

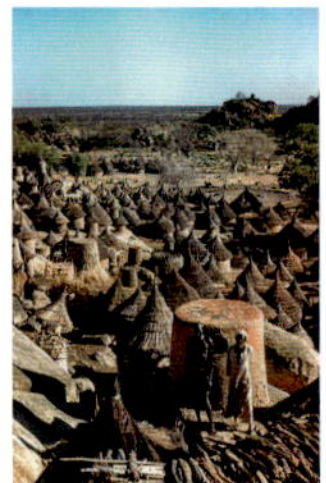

6

General view of the village of Kao in the Kao-Nyaro area. 1949

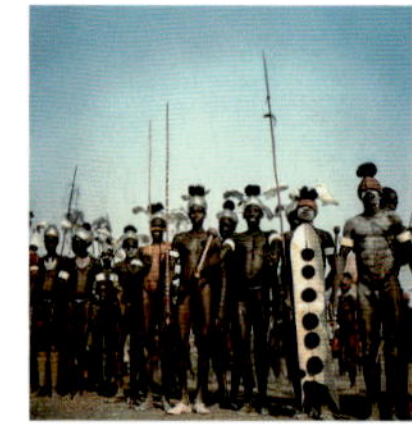

7

Young warriors await the Latuka Dance of the Rainmakers ceremony to begin. 1948

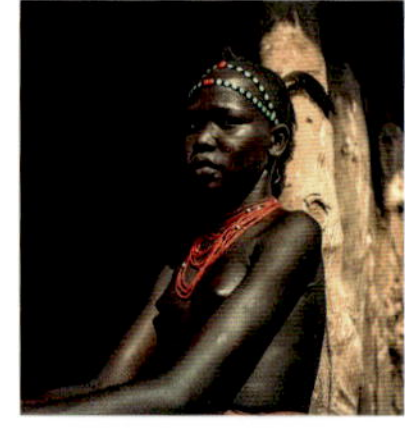

9

Dinka girl dressed for a ceremonial dance. 1949

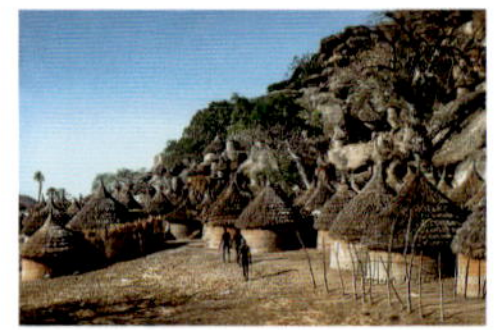

10–11

General view of the village of Kao in the Kao-Nyaro area. 1949

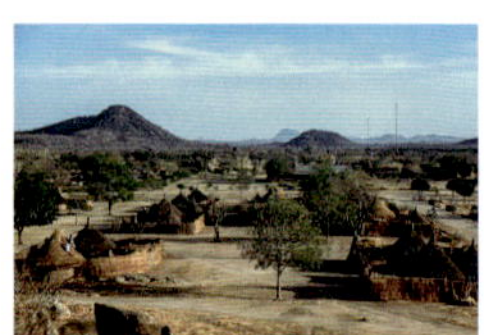

12

General view of the village of Kao in the Kao-Nyaro area. 1949

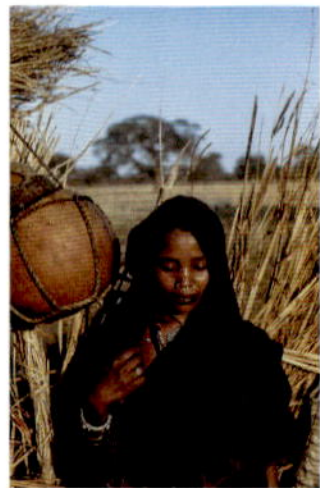

13

A girl of the Aulad Himeid in the village of Kao. 1949

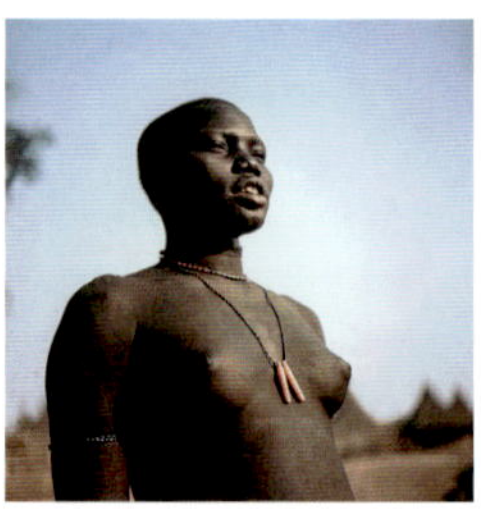

14

Portrait of a young Latuka girl. 1948

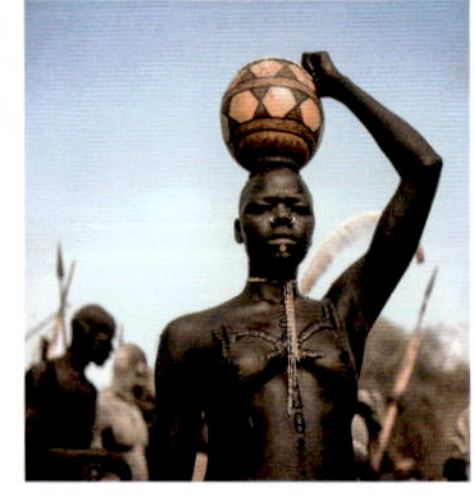

15

Korongo Nuba girl. Cicatrice designs on her chest are made in childhood by cutting the flesh and rubbing in wood ash. The gourd contains local beer. 1949

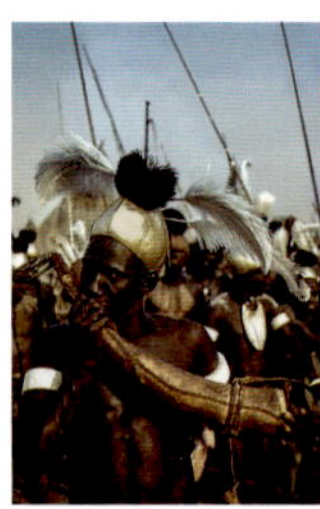

16

A warrior sounds the native horn (namogo), which is an elephant's tusk covered with uncut stretched oxtail skin. 1948

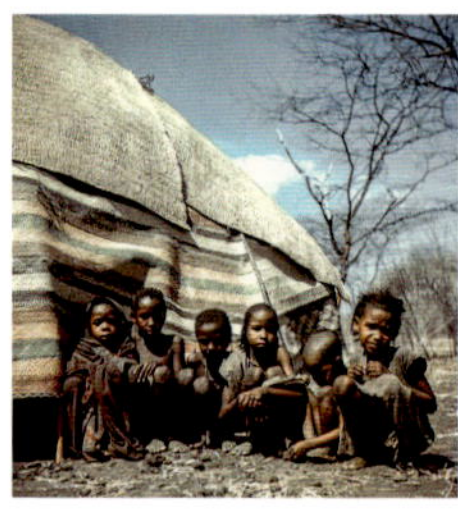

17

Children of the Aulad Himeid Baggara. 1949

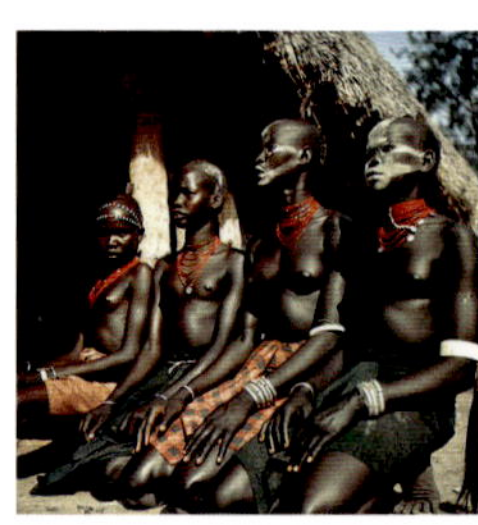

19

Dinka and Nuer girls dressed for a ceremonial dance. 1949

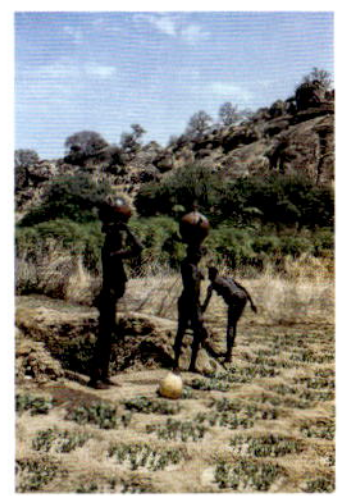

20

Mesakin Quasi women watering tobacco plants. Tobacco is smoked, chewed and powdered into snuff. 1949

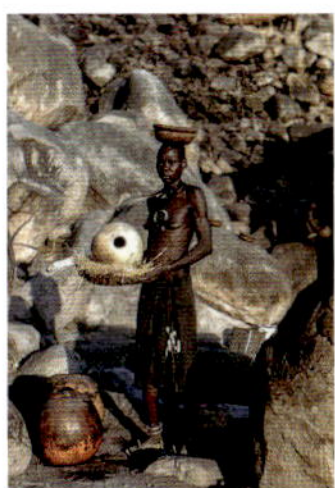

21

Collecting water from a well two and a half miles from the village of Kao. 1949

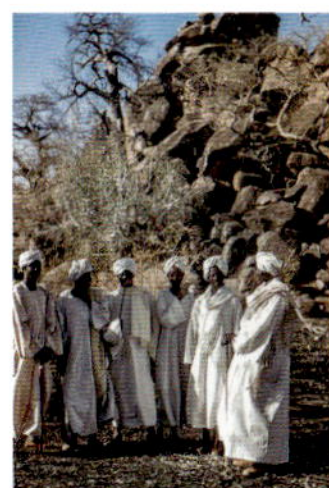

23

Chieftains of the Koalib, with their chief at Delami. 1949

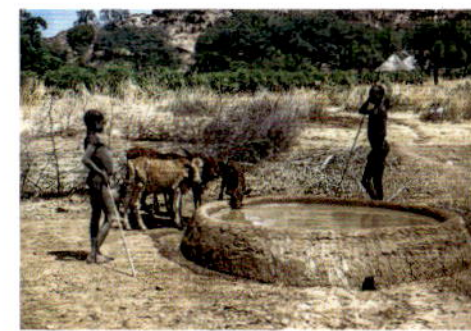

24

Children tending to the cattle. 1949

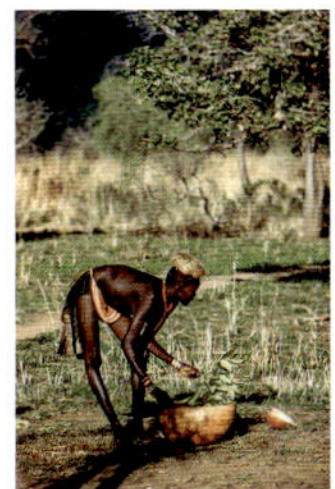

25

Mesakin Quasi woman tending to the tobacco plants. 1949

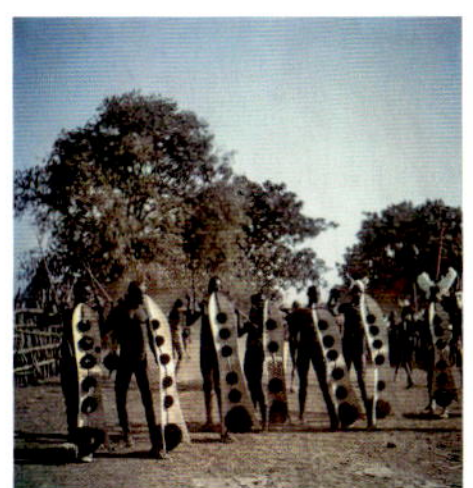

27

Young warriors await the Latuka Dance of the Rainmakers ceremony to begin. 1948

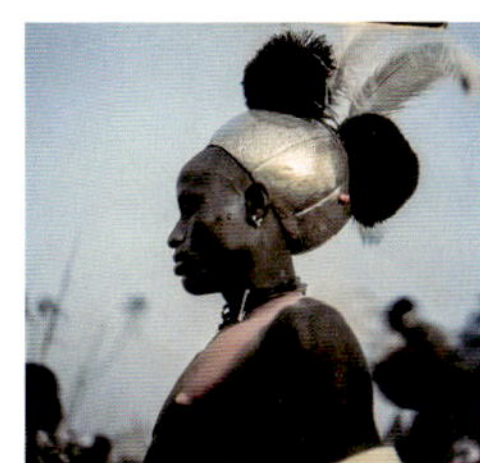

28

Portrait of a Latuka warrior dressed for the ceremony with a brass helmet decorated with ostrich breast feathers and crane quills. 1948

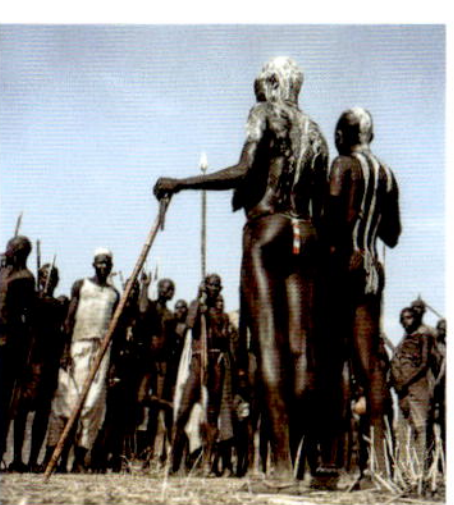

29

Young warriors await the Dance of the Rainmakers ceremony to begin. 1948

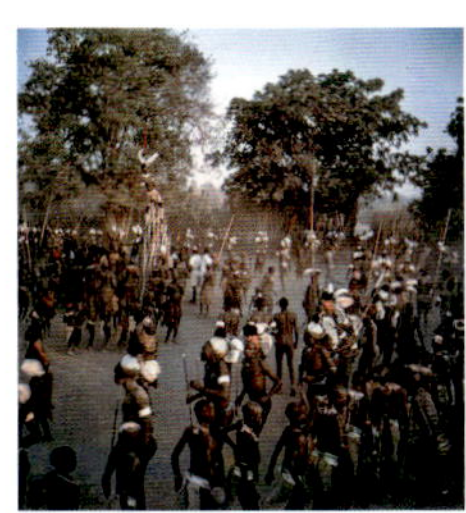

30

The Dance of the Rainmakers. 1948

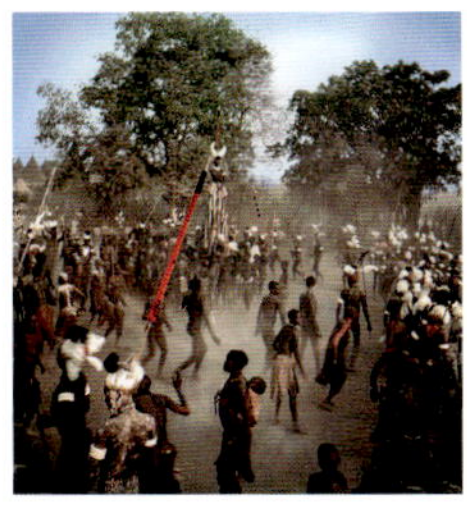

31

The Dance of the Rainmakers. 1948

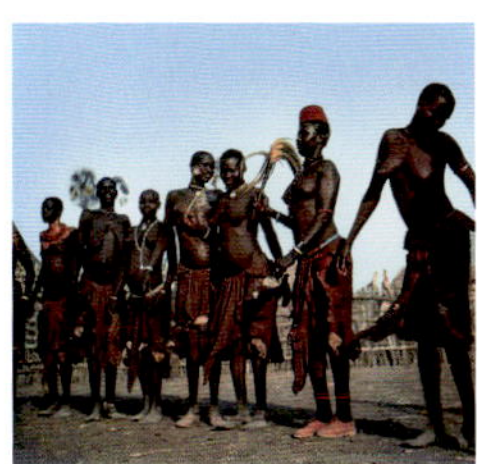

33

Women of the village chant tribal songs. 1948

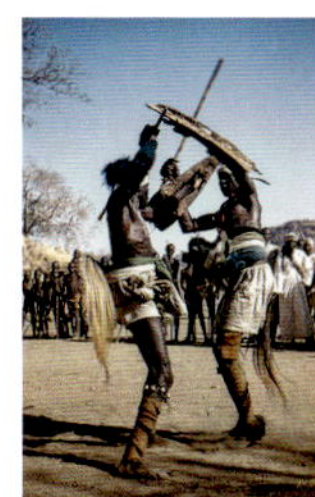

34

Stick fighters of the Mesakin Tiwal tribe. The sticks are about three feet long with rawhide handles and the shield is made of buffalo hide. 1949

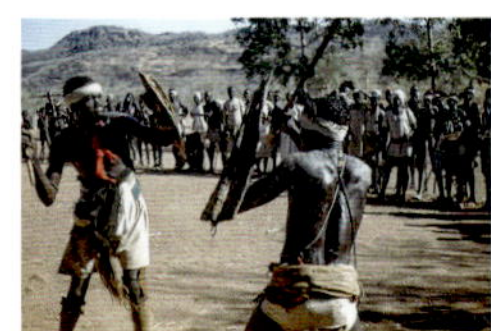

35

Stick fighters of the Mesakin Tiwal tribe. 1949

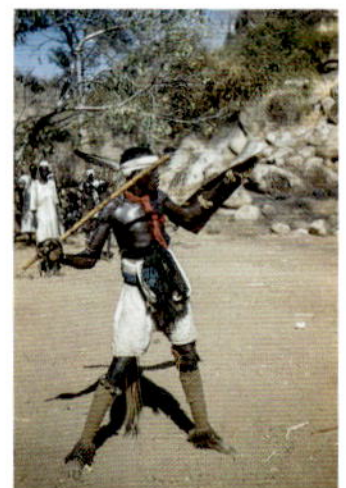

36

Stick fighter of the Mesakin Tiwal tribe. 1949

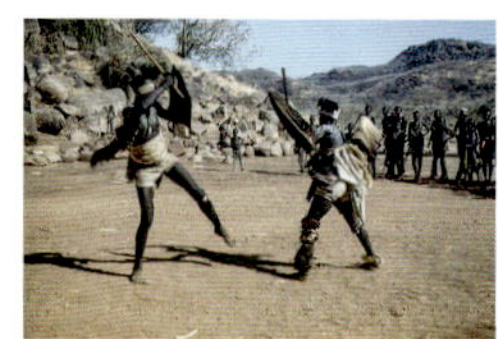

37

Stick fighters of the Mesakin Tiwal tribe. 1949

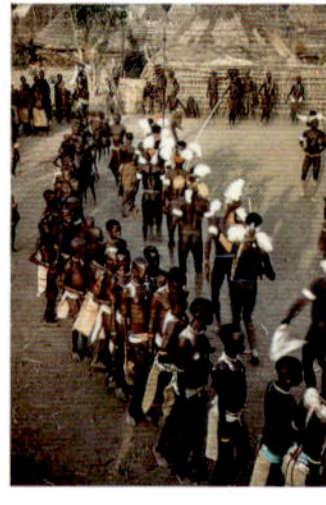

38

Girls line up to join the Latuka Dance of the Rainmakers. 1948

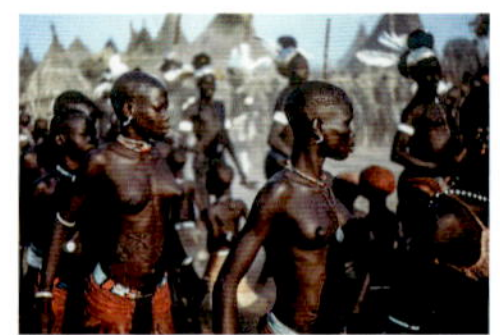

39

Girls line up to join the Dance of the Rainmakers. 1948

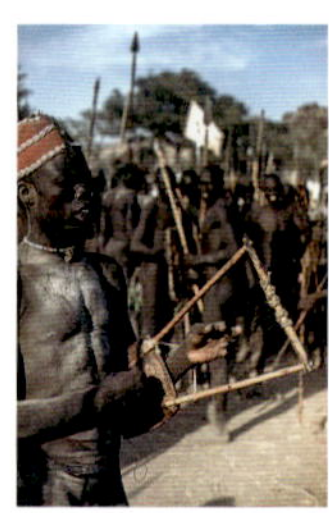

40

A Korongo Nuba plays a lyre-type harp called the rababa. 1949

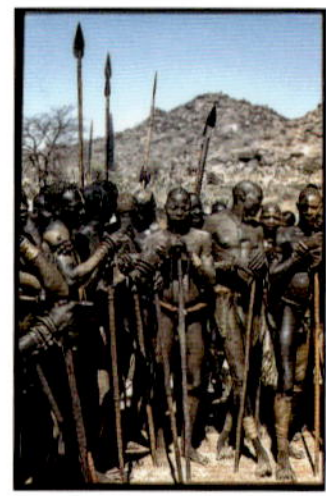

41

Bracelet fighters of the Kao-Nyaro. The lethal brass bracelets used by the fighters weigh up to two kilos and have two-inch double flanges. 1949

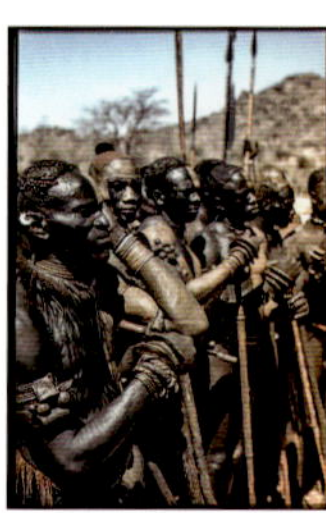

43

Bracelet fighters of the Kao-Nyaro. 1949

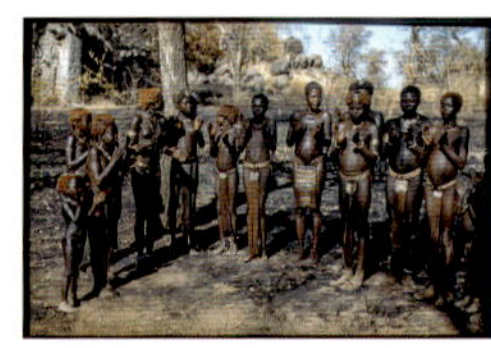

44

Women of the Koalib Nuba from Delami. Their hair is matted with red clay and sim-sim oil. 1949

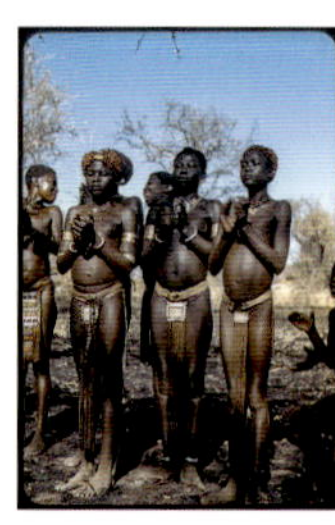

45

Women of the Koalib Nuba from Delami. 1949

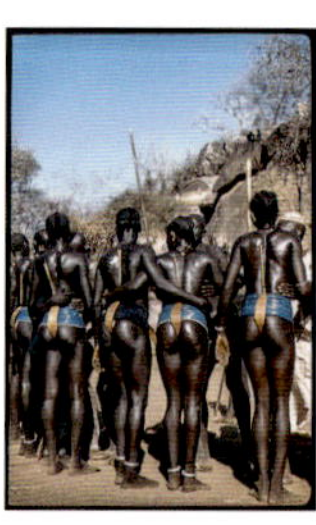

47

Girls of the Mesakin Tiwal. 1949

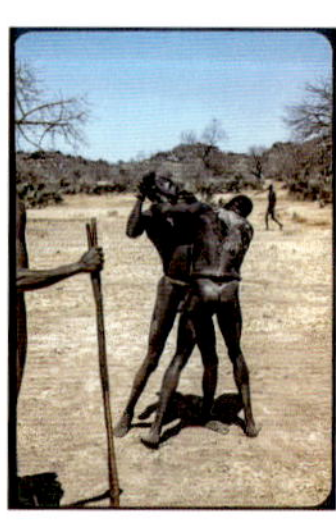

48

Bracelet fighters of the Kao-Nyaro. 1949

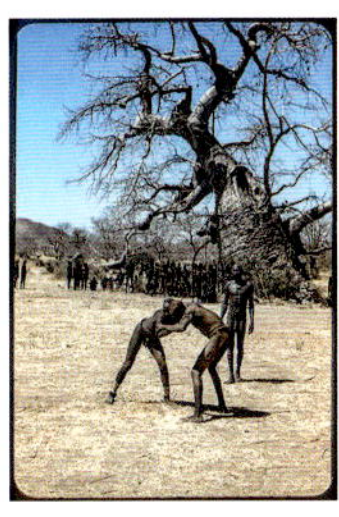

49

Bracelet fighters of the Kao-Nyaro. 1949

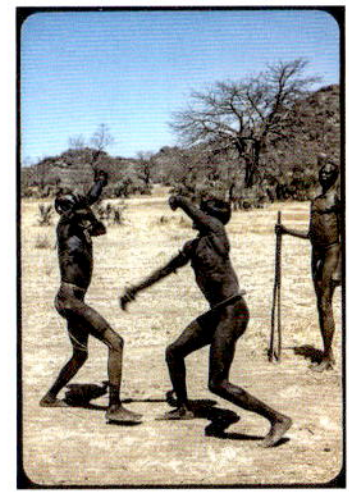

50

Bracelet fighters of the Kao-Nyaro. 1949

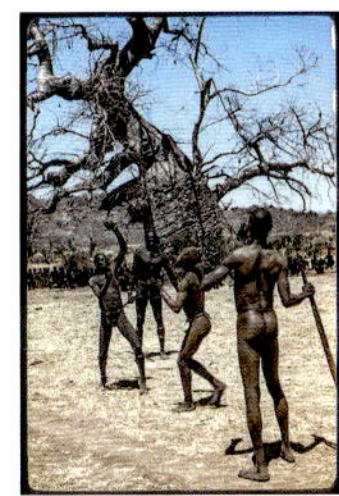

51

Bracelet fighters of the Kao-Nyaro. 1949

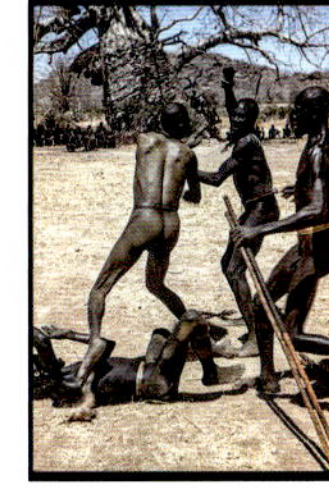

52

Bracelet fighters of the Kao-Nyaro. 1949

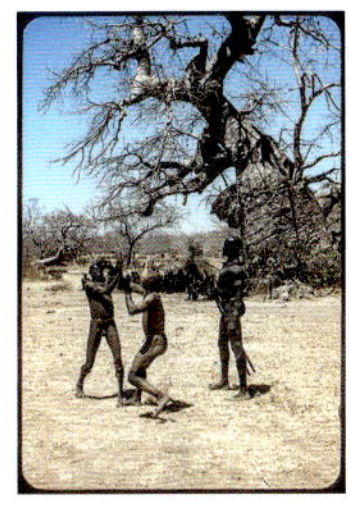

53

Bracelet fighters of the Kao-Nyaro. 1949

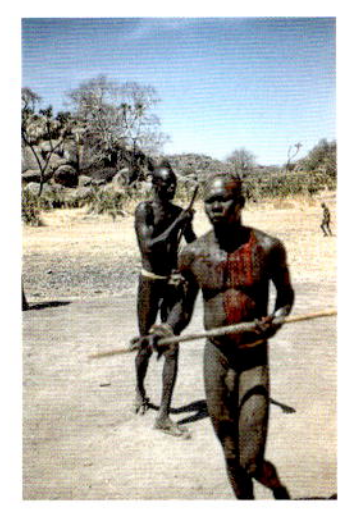

55

Stick fighters of the Kao-Nyaro. 1949

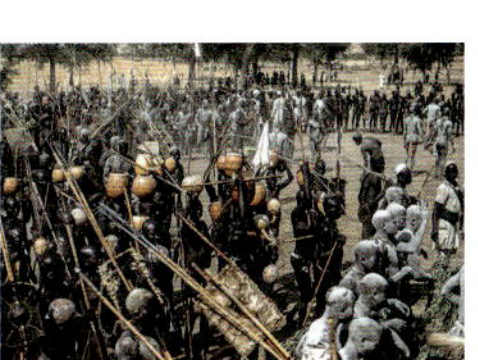

56

At the beginning of the gathering, or sibr, young wrestlers of the Korongo Nuba gather together before the fighting bouts take place. 1949

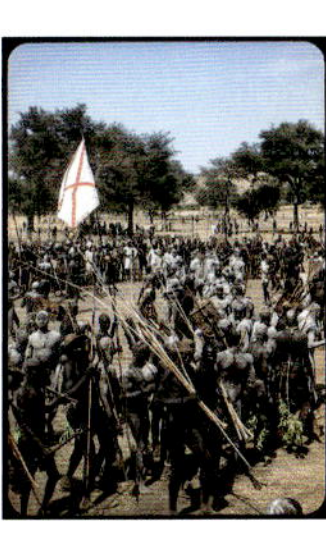

57

At the beginning of the sibr. 1949

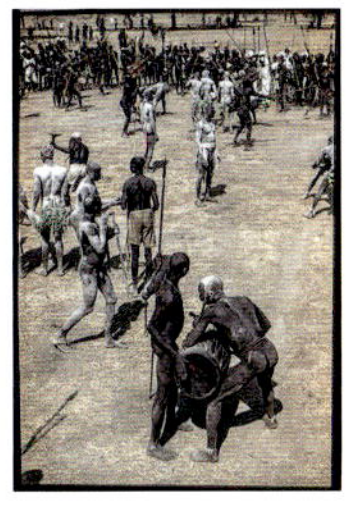

59

At the beginning of the sibr. 1949

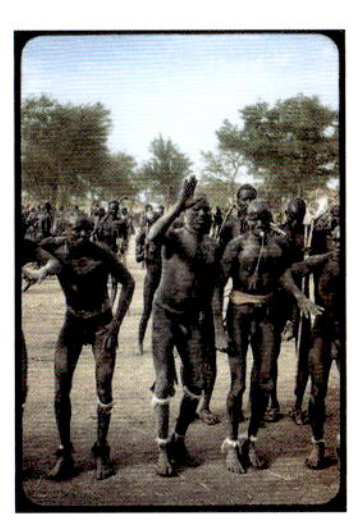

60

Nuba tribesmen pride themselves as wrestlers. They are powdered in ash so they can get a grip on each other's bodies during a wrestling match. 1949

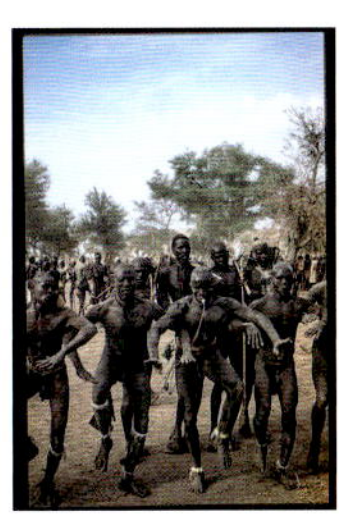

61

Nuba tribesmen wrestlers. 1949

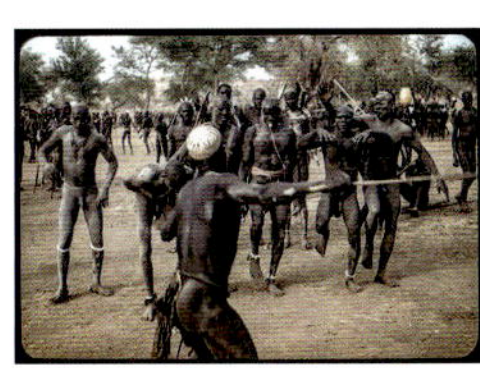

62–63

Nuba tribesmen wrestlers. 1949

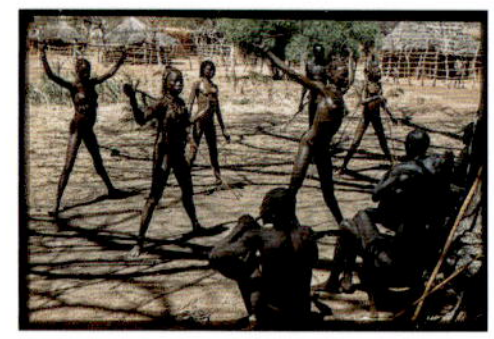

64

Girl dancers of the village of Sao perform to the drums in front of the young men of the tribe who will be fighting for them. 1949

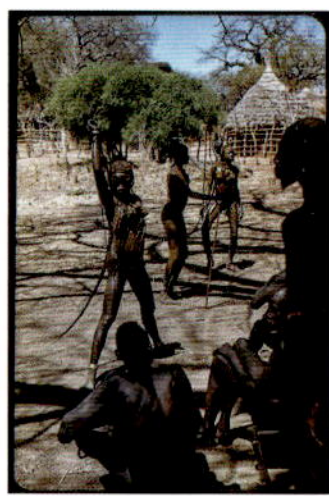

65

Girl dancers of the village of Sao. 1949

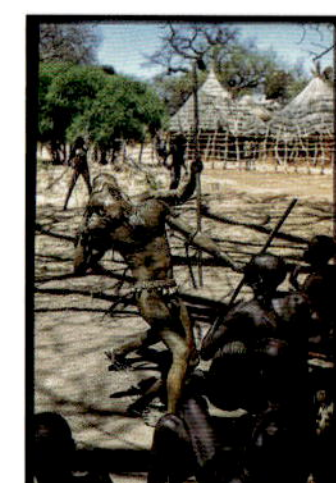

67

Young men imitate the call of the fish eagle before a fight. 1949

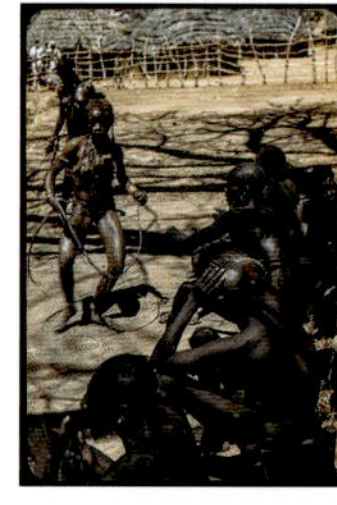

68

Girl dancers of the village of Sao. 1949

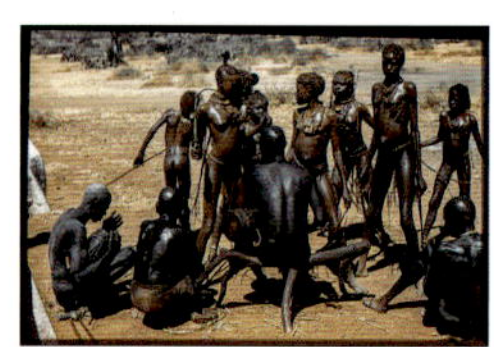

69

Girl dancers of the village of Sao. 1949

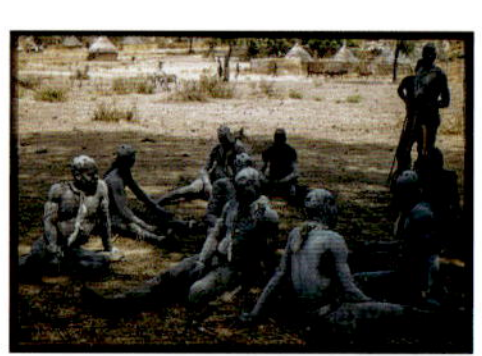

70–71

Powdered in wood ash, wrestlers of the Korongo Nuba wait to take part in a match. 1949

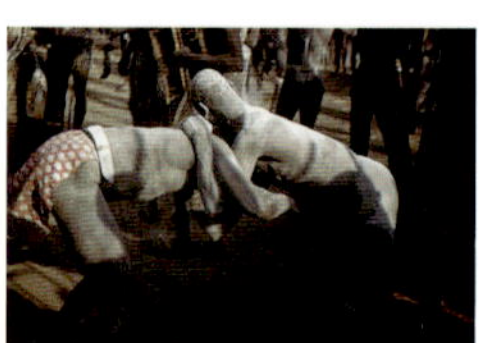

72

Wrestlers of the Kao-Nyaro. 1949

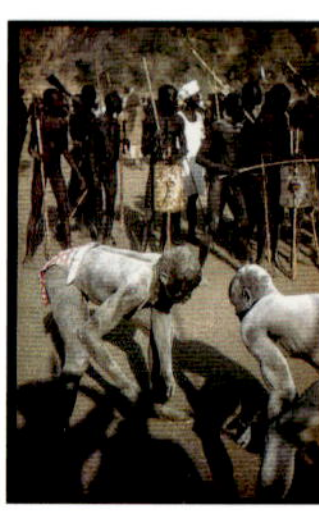

73

Wrestlers of the Kao-Nyaro. 1949

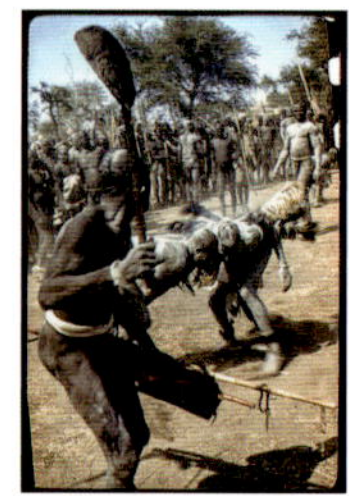

75

Wrestlers of the Kao-Nyaro. 1949

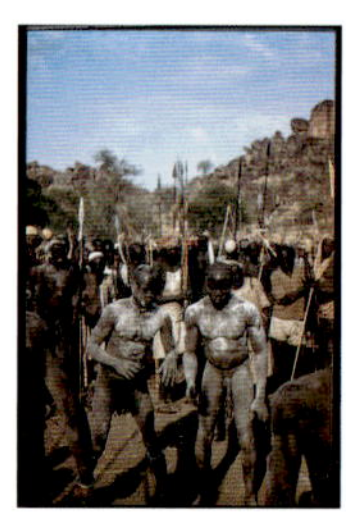

76

Wrestlers of the Kao-Nyaro. 1949

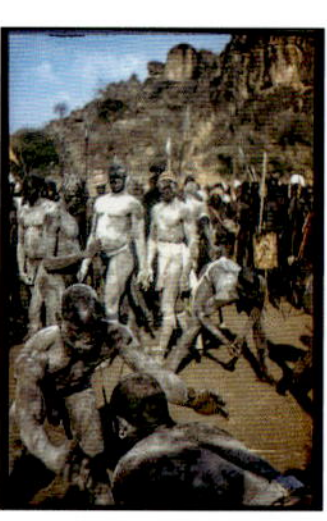

77

Wrestlers of the Kao-Nyaro. 1949

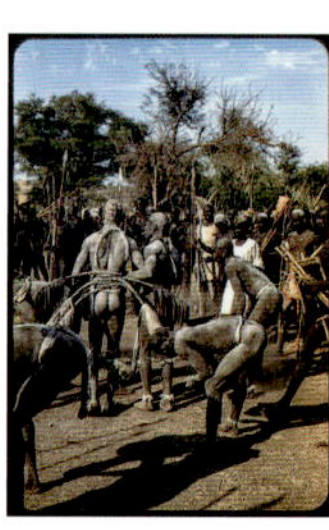

79

Wrestlers of the Kao-Nyaro. 1949

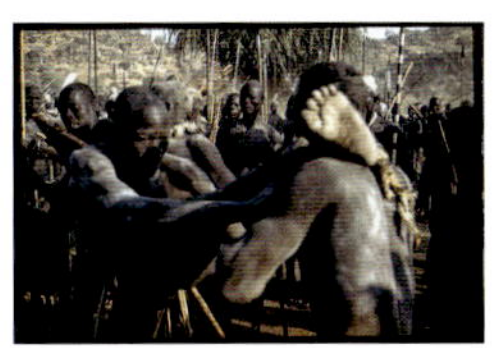

80

Wrestlers of the Kao-Nyaro. 1949

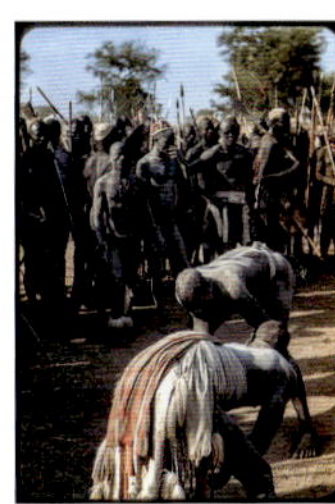

81

Wrestlers of the Kao-Nyaro. 1949

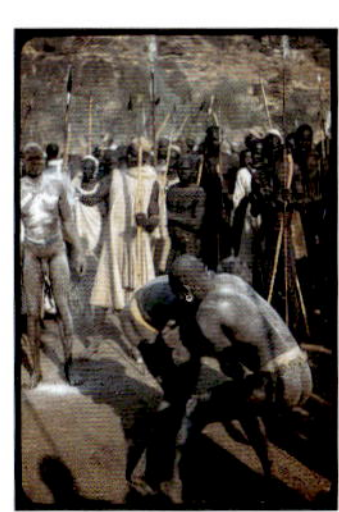

83

Wrestlers of the Kao-Nyaro. 1949

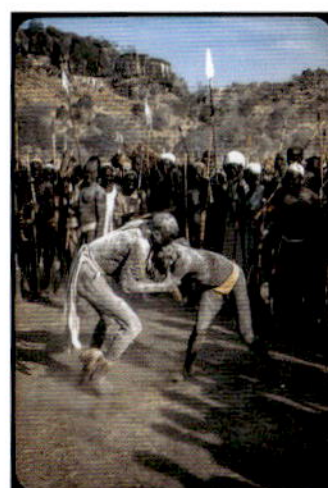

84

Wrestlers of the Kao-Nyaro. 1949

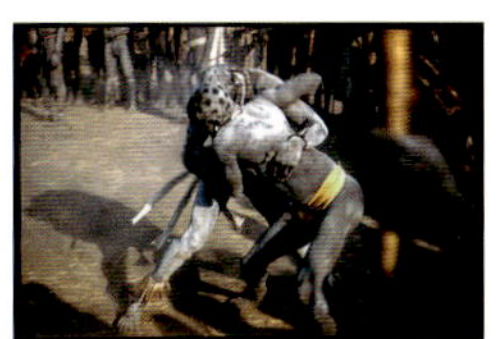

85

Wrestlers of the Kao-Nyaro. 1949

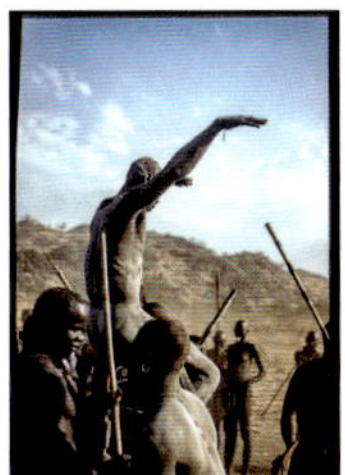

87

The champion of a Korongo Nuba wrestling match is carried shoulder high, what is known as the chairing of the victor. 1949

THE SUDAN IN COLOUR

Chris Steele-Perkins

Why do photographers do what they do: work on this project rather than another?

•

I had no particular interest in Africa before I actually went there. It did not hold my imagination like Latin America and Lebanon did in my earlier photographic days. I first went on assignment to Africa for an Italian illustrated encyclopaedia of the natural wonders of the world. The wonders I had to photograph, in colour, were the Victoria Falls and Lake Victoria. At that time I had this idea that my serious work was shot in black and white and that colour was more commercial, less serious. The photographers I admired, many from Magnum, including George Rodger, Henri Cartier-Bresson, René Burri, amongst many more, all worked in black and white. Fortunately I was able to leave this prejudice behind, but at the time I approached the assignment as a commercial travel shoot, not expecting it to be an encounter that changed my life. By the time I had finished my work in Africa, I felt Africa calling me back. It had slipped into my bloodstream and become a compulsion that brought me back and back again over a period of more than thirty years. Why photograph Africa and not somewhere else? Because it felt almost like I had no choice. It was what I had to do.

•

As a middle-class product of a private school and a sheltered, small-town English upbringing, Africa was about as far away from my experience and understanding of the world as could be, and as such the reason I became a photographer: to unleash myself into the world, explore and discover its wonders and secrets and to live a life that aspired to be free.

•

George too had gone to Africa out of need: a need to find a world that stood in contrast to the mass-industrialized human butchery he had been photographing during the Second World War, a need for another Eden.

Yet even at the heart of the Nuba was a ritual of violence in the organized combat and then a future of persecution by the Sudanese state.

•

Africa has captured the imagination of many artists and many of the Magnum photographers have followed different routes into Africa to find or to bury different demons and to be nourished by that source. George too was to return to Africa, but, despite efforts to do so and his own deep disappointments, he never got back to his source, the Nuba. However, some of them sought him out and found him in his home in Kent. In 1993, the last time I saw George in his home, he was being visited by Nuba Mountain Solidarity, a campaign organized to fight persecution of the Nuba people by the Sudanese government. They were poring through his photographs from 1949. It was a poignant reminder of the value of great photography that can speak from the past and yet stamp its authority on the present, not just for the journalists, publishers, academics, photography community, but also those whose lives are depicted in the photographs, who value them because the photographer cared, showed due respect, and made a longstanding record of their way of life, and for that they were thankful.

•

It seems appropriate that in Magnum Photos' seventieth year, after seventy years of turmoil and fellowship, the "lost" colour photographs of George should be published, to celebrate this seminal work on the Nuba, Latuka and other Sudanese peoples and also remind us that this is the Magnum that George had co-founded seven decades ago, a Magnum that is still very much alive and can surprise with these archive treasures misplaced by history.

•

As we rediscover the work of this modest and honourable Scotsman, bear in mind that these photographs, with their humanity and beauty that forge experience and empathy into an emotional and aesthetic achievement, embody qualities that should still resonate through the work of Magnum photographers to this day.

O child of man . . .

. . .

Thy sense is clogg'd with dull mortality,
Thy spirit fetter'd with the bond of clay;
Open thine eyes and see.

Alfred Lord Tennyson, "Timbuctoo", 1929

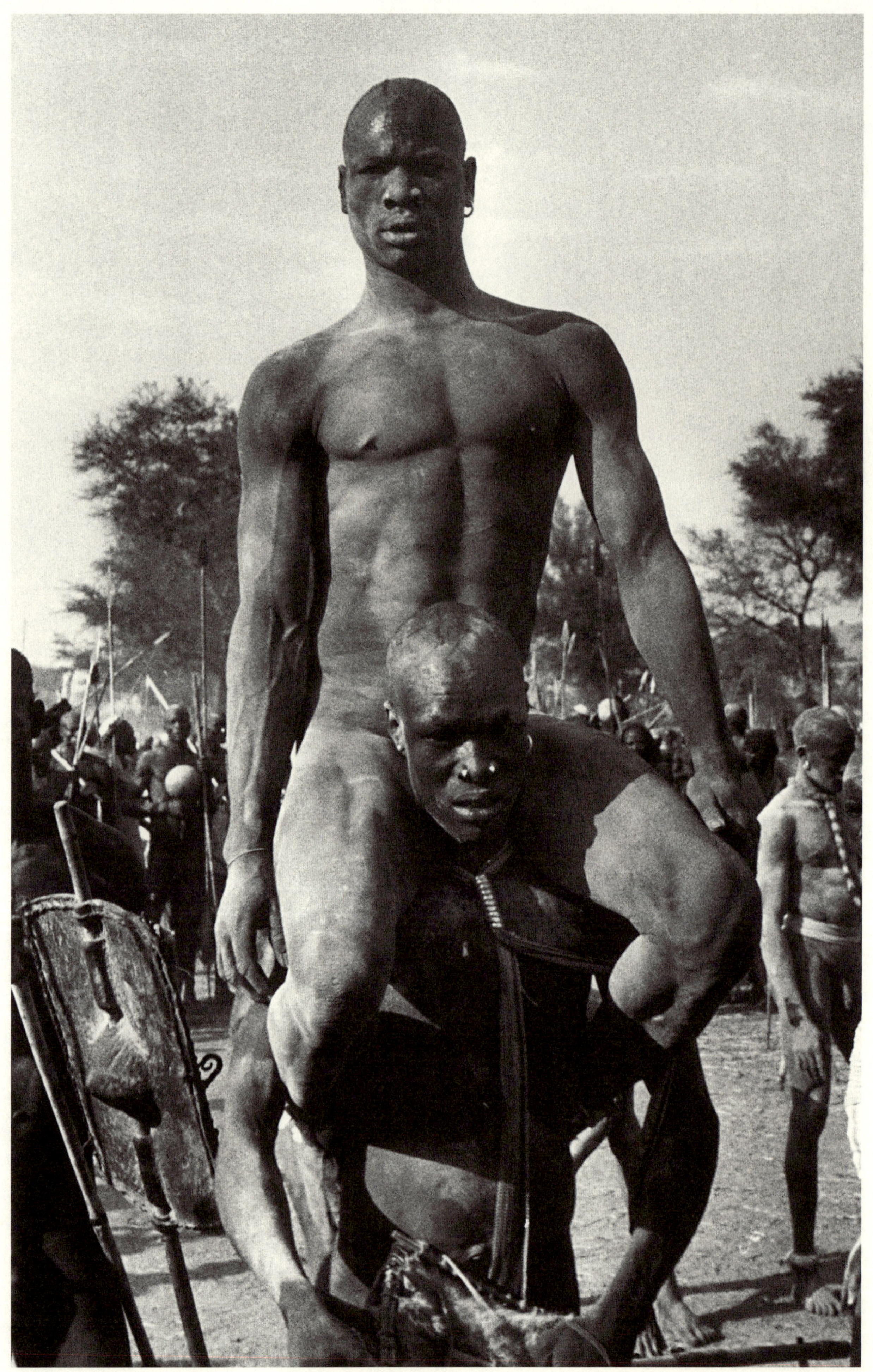

THE COLOUR PHOTOGRAPHS BY GEORGE RODGER

Aaron Schuman

It is well established that the beautiful and beguiling black-and-white photographs made by George Rodger in 1948 and 1949—most famously of the indigenous people of the Nuba mountains, in the former central Sudanese province of Kordofan, and the Latuka and other tribes of southern Sudan—are some of the most historically important and influential images taken in sub-Saharan Africa during the twentieth century. Not only do they represent an array of tribes who were thoroughly unique and steadfastly traditional in terms of their customs, costumes, architecture, agriculture, rituals and social gatherings; they also document these tribes' first authorized encounter with a Western photographer, as Rodger was granted official permission to photograph there by the Sudanese government itself. Of course, Rodger was genuinely fascinated by the people and cultures he encountered, but as a founding member of the newly established Magnum Photos and an active contributor to the rapidly expanding international mass media at the time, he was also determined to fully convey and share his experiences of the Nuba with the rest of the world via the then dominant medium of photography.

•

One of the most familiar, powerful and iconic of all of Rodger's photographs depicts a victorious Korongo Nuba wrestler being carried through a crowd, on the shoulders of his defeated opponent. The subject's posture is impressively dominant and proud. Furthermore, rendered in black and white, his body—dusted with white wood ash and naked apart from two small nose rings, a thin bracelet on his right wrist and a hoop earring in his left ear—appears solid and heavy, the varying grey tones of each muscle and vein mimicking the smooth monochromatic contours of expertly chiselled marble. His expression is more ambiguous though, both profoundly authoritative and intensely curious, and because of deep shadows that fall across his eyes in many reproductions of the image, it often appears as if he is staring directly down Rodger's lens (when in fact, on closer inspection of finer prints, it becomes clear that he is gazing intently over the head of the photographer). This forthright encounter, between the photographer and his subject as well as between the viewer and the photograph itself, is one that is both immediate and mesmerizing. Yet, as the representatives of these two seemingly disparate cultures face off—and furthermore, as the instant itself is captured on film and then circulated throughout the world again and again, both contemporarily and then subsequently for many generations to come—what exactly it shows, and what it ultimately signifies, isn't entirely as straightforward as at first it may seem.

•

Amongst a wide variety of interpretations, the photograph can—and often has—been too easily misconstrued as one situated within the long-standing colonial tradition of representing the people of Africa as "noble savages"; as specimens of a "primitive" humanity untouched by "civilization". Yet, it is important to recognize that directly prior to photographing the Nuba peoples, Rodger had spent the previous decade—from 1939 to 1947—as a Second World War correspondent for *Life* magazine. In that time, he had covered the death and destruction experienced during the London Blitz, the brutality of the Burma campaign, the Allies' violent progress through Italy, and finally the horrific piles of corpses and desperately emaciated survivors discovered at the Bergen-Belsen concentration camp after its liberation in 1945, as well as much more. Throughout Europe and the rest of the world, Rodger had already borne witness to a level of savagery almost beyond the scope of the imagination. With this in mind, one suspects that upon encountering the Nuba he saw himself photographing something that was certainly noble but not savage, a sophisticated and civilized rather than "primitive" culture in which conflict was resolved via refereed hand-to-hand combat, and in which the victor was lifted aloft, paraded around and celebrated by the man whom he himself had defeated. As Rodger wrote several years later, "When we came to leave the Nuba Jebels [mountains] we took with us only memories of a people ... so much more hospitable, chivalrous and gracious than many of us who live in the 'Dark Continents' outside Africa."[1] Looking again at Rodger's famous monochrome image of this wrestling champion, it is vital to remember that such photographs — despite their first impressions — are not always so black and white.

•

Today, much has been written and learned about the Nuba, due in large part to Rodger's photographs (which first appeared in *National Geographic* in 1951) as well as to the subsequent and extensive photographic study, *The Last of the Nuba*, published in the early 1970s by Leni Riefenstahl, who herself credited Rodger's famous image of the wrestling champion as the catalyst for her own work, stating, "The artistic style of the picture, together with the expressive power of the two black Nuba, fascinated me so much that from then on I never lost my interest in this tribe. This picture changed my life."[2] Yet, until now, what often distinguished Riefenstahl's imagery from that of Rodger's (apart from the fact that they were made several decades later; "ten years too late" according to a Kordofan police chief that Riefenstahl met during her initial search for the Nuba) was that they were printed and published in vividly striking colour. Here, in *Nuba & Latuka: The Colour Photographs*, we revisit Rodger's original 1948 and 1949 trips through a distinctly different and unfamiliar spectrum; through the unknown and previously unpublished colour images that he made alongside his more famous black-and-white work. What these images reveal, apart from an added visual vibrancy, are fascinating clues into the working practices of a professional photographer at the top of his game in the mid-twentieth century.

•

Returning to the victorious wrestler for a final time, in *Nuba & Latuka: The Colour Photographs* we catch another glimpse of him, but in doing so quite literally gain an entirely new perspective on the subject. In this instance, having been carried past Rodger, we see our hero from the side, surrounded by his fellow tribesmen and watched from afar by the tribeswomen, as he gracefully raises his arms into a pale blue sky, echoing the contours of the rolling ochre hills in the distance. Although not quite as immediate as the previously known photograph in terms of conveying the power and presence of the subject himself, this colour picture—with its palette of pastel yellows, browns and blues—seems to offer a new-found sense of and insight into the event's overall atmosphere; the sunlight is warm, the air dusty and golden, and one can almost feel its soft touch and smell its dry earthiness as it rises from beneath the marching men's feet and drifts on by. Rather than directly describing or documenting the moment itself as it unfolds, the picture's subtle hues evoke a powerful mood, enriching and saturating the viewer's experience of the moment with details that stretch beyond the descriptive, and the image introduces a subtle sense of environment and place as well as the people it depicts.

•

The timing of the image suggests that, in the moment, Rodger prioritized shooting in black and white, but having secured his now iconic photograph, he then reached for a second Leica draped around his neck which was loaded with Kodachrome film, in order to capture the event in colour as well. (Comparison between other colour photographs collected here and their black-and-white counterparts also suggests that Rodger's working pattern was to first shoot in black and white and then follow up with colour). In fact, it was during these trips that Rodger first began to experiment with colour; this was not only an important aesthetic decision but also a canny commercial one.

•

Less than two years earlier, Rodger—along with photographers Robert Capa, Henri Cartier-Bresson, David "Chim" Seymour, Bill Vandivert and others—had founded Magnum Photos Inc., a cooperative photographic agency intent on collectively supporting its members and protecting their copyrights as well as efficiently distributing and selling their work internationally. In order to gain coverage of the entire globe, Capa suggested that each Magnum photographer focus on a particular region, with Cartier-Bresson assigned to South and East Asia, Seymour and Vandivert to Europe and America, and Rodger to the Middle East and Africa (with Capa roaming the world wherever the stories took him). And in fact, alongside the original 1947 Magnum Agreement, accountancy records housed today in Rodger's own archive—overseen by his wife,

Jinx, and still located in the small darkroom that Rodger himself built on the ground floor of his rambling cottage in Kent in the late 1950s (which continues to emit the faint odour of photographic fixer more than twenty years after his passing)—reveal that Rodger was in fact the agency's highest earner in its early years. In Magnum's first five months, he had brought $3,687.78 into the agency, substantially more than Capa's $2,323.43, and more than six times as much as Cartier-Bresson's $555.20. As Rodger was aware, although prominent periodicals such as *Life* and *Picture Post* hadn't yet entirely embraced it, by the late 1940s the editorial photography market was shifting steadily towards colour photography, with magazines such as *National Geographic*, *Ladies' Home Journal* (which frequently commissioned stories from Magnum's founding members) and many more regularly demanding colour as well as black-and-white pictures. It's clear that these early and previously unpublished colour images were in fact an attempt on Rodger's part to cater to an evolving marketplace as well as to his own evolving vision.

•

Additionally, as his wife Jinx recalls, alongside his two Leicas Rodger would also regularly carry a medium-format Rolleiflex camera which he would use to shoot "cover images" for the potential magazines that might buy his stories. In this book we discover an intriguing variety of these carefully composed, square images, mostly portraits of women and children, many of which contain a distinctively different palette due to the fact that they were shot on the less archival film stock Ektachrome, and have thus deteriorated substantially over the years. But again, the presence of such pictures within this archive, which both technically and aesthetically take the demands of the market into great consideration, further suggests how invested Rodger was in making both visually captivating and commercially viable work.

•

That said, in 1948 colour-film technology was itself still only in its relative infancy. Despite many successful experiments and the invention of various promising processes since the mid-nineteenth century, the rendering of realistic colour photographs remained prohibitively expensive, often unreliable and frustratingly unstable well into the twentieth century (as exemplified by Rodger's own medium-format Ektachrome work). The earliest product to bear the Kodachrome name was invented in 1913, and released commercially to the motion-picture industry in 1915, yet it relied upon a complicated two-colour process (using only red and green filters, which meant that blues were often poorly reproduced) that limited its market substantially. It was only in 1935, when Eastman Kodak released a newly developed "integral tri-pack" version of Kodachrome, that accurate, dependable and archival colour photography became affordable and accessible to both professional photographers and the public at large.

•

Looking at many of the most popular periodicals of the day, it's clear to see that by the late 1940s colour photography had finally seeped deeply into the visual consciousness of print media, particularly within the realms of fashion and advertising; furthermore, amateur photographers were using Kodachrome widely. Yet within Rodger's circle and the general contexts of documentary and reportage photography, black-and-white imagery still reigned supreme, partly due to the public's longstanding familiarity with it, and partly due to the continued limitations of colour technology. Kodachrome—with all of its rich tones and sultry saturations—was only produced with an ISO of 10 at the time; even under intense sunlight or powerful artificial lights, photographers using the film would need to adapt to relatively long exposures and wide apertures, or would require a sturdy tripod or relatively stationary subjects, in order to get an accurate and stable image—all of which would prove challenging for those practitioners who hand-held their cameras, and responded quickly and spontaneously to the ever-shifting "decisive moments" and events around them. Looking at Rodger's own colour images of the Nuba and Latuka, it's obvious that even under the midday sub-Saharan sun he was working with limited ranges when it came to shutter speed and depth of field. Nevertheless, in many of these images Rodger used this to his advantage—with both foreground and background falling out of focus, he propels us as viewers into the scene where details are at their sharpest, with the blurred feet of dancers, sweeping streaks of wrestlers' limbs, and the dusty clouds of kicked-up earth surrounding our vision and interjecting a new-found energy to the experience. Rodger's use of Kodachrome not only adds a vibrancy to the scene in terms of colour but also a vividness in terms of both movement and the overall moment, where the immediacy of his vision and the spontaneity of his camerawork are fully captured and conveyed as well.

•

Until relatively recently, the standard historical narrative within photographic circles was that William Eggleston's exhibition *Color Photographs*, held at the Museum of Modern Art (MoMA) in New York in 1976—and the accompanying book, *William Eggleston's Guide* (published by MoMA the same year)—heralded the beginning of legitimate, artistic colour photography. Such a mythology was promoted strongly by the museum's own original press release for the show:

> Unlike most of their predecessors, whose color work has been either formless or too pretty, a new generation of young photographers has begun to use color in a confident spirit of freedom and naturalness. In their work the role of color is more than simply descriptive or decorative, and assumes a central place in the definition of the picture's content… For Eggleston, as for others in the new generation of color photographers, color is [as John Szarkowski writes] "existential and descriptive; these pictures are not photographs of color, any more than they are photographs of shapes, textures, objects, symbols, or events, but rather photographs of experience, as it has been ordered and clarified within the structures imposed by the camera."[3]

Throughout the twenty-first century this resilient yet erroneous narrative has been continually questioned, contradicted and rewritten thanks to the resurfacing of a hidden history full of unrecognized work by accomplished photographers, all of whom were clearly committed to exploring the possibilities of colour photography beyond the "descriptive and decorative", and using it "in a confident spirit of freedom and naturalness" all their own long before the 1970s. Saul Leiter's extensive colour catalogue from the 1940s and 1950s came to prominence through several exhibitions at the Howard Greenberg Gallery in the late 1990s and the publication of *Early Color* in 2006; Helen Levitt's colour work from the 1960s and 1970s, although exhibited as a slide show at MoMA two years before Eggleston's infamous exhibition, gained much wider attention and appreciation when they featured in her magnum opus, *Crosstown*, published in 2001; key selections from the one hundred rolls of Kodachrome that Garry Winogrand's shot during his 1964 Guggenheim-funded American road trip first appeared as a considered and strikingly accomplished portfolio in his posthumous book *1964*, published in 2002; Fred Herzog's extensive collection of colour slides, focusing on working-class Vancouver during the 1950s and 1960s, finally received recognition when a major retrospective of his work was staged at the Vancouver Art Gallery in 2007. And of course, alongside these few examples there are hundreds if not thousands of equally important, challenging and fascinating bodies of twentieth-century colour work by many other photographers still out there, all of whom could claim a legitimate and important place within this emerging history.

•

With that in mind, in addition to offering new-found insight into Rodger's encounters with these now famous tribes in 1949, this book firmly situates George Rodger within this burgeoning and important field of photographic history. Here his work in Sudan, as well as his photographic practice in general, gains even more poignancy, power and relevance as a new and dynamic dimension of his work is revealed. These photographs help to further expose Rodger's committed professionalism—his dedication to his own subjects, his practice, his clientele, his agency and his audience—and finally bring to light his incredible ability to capture both events and environments via the camera no matter what type of film it contained. As colourful as these newfound photographs may be, ultimately "these pictures are not photographs of color... but rather photographs of experience".

1 George Rodger, *The Village of the Nubas* [1955], London 1999, p. 112.

2 Leni Riefenstahl, *The Last of the Nuba* [1973], London 1976, p. 10.

3 "Color Photographs by William Eggleston at the Museum of Modern Art", Press release, 25 May, 1976, available at https://www.moma.org/momaorg/shared//pdfs/docs/press_archives/5391/releases/MOMA_1976_0051_40.pdf.

A member of Verlagsgruppe Random House GmbH
Neumarkter Straße 28 · 81673 Munich

Front cover image: The champion of a Korongo Nuba wrestling match. See page 87

Page 102: The champion of a Korongo Nuba wrestling match in a black-and-white image from 1949.

Prestel Publishing Ltd.
14–17 Wells Street
London W1T 3PD

Prestel Publishing
900 Broadway, Suite 603
New York, NY 10003

Library of Congress Control Number is available; British Library Cataloguing-in-Publication Data: a catalogue record for this book is available from the British Library

Editorial direction: Curt Holtz
Copy-editing: Jonathan Fox
Design and layout: Hannah Feldmeier
Production management: Corinna Pickart
Separations: Reproline Mediateam, Munich
Printing and binding: TBB, a.s., Banská Bystrica
Paper: Primasilk, EOS

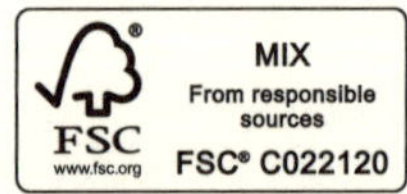

Verlagsgruppe Random House FSC® N001967

Printed in Slovakia
ISBN 978-3-7913-8322-4

www.prestel.com